MAIWA'S REVENGE

H. RIDER HAGGARD

WILDSIDE PRESS

CONTENTS.

MAIWA'S REVENGE.

CHAPTER I.

GOBO STRIKES.

ONE day—it was about a week after Allan
Quatermain told me his story of the "Three
Lions" and of the moving death of Jim-Jim—
he and I were walking home together on the
termination of a day's shooting. He had about
two thousand acres of shooting round the place
he bought in Yorkshire, over a hundred of
which were wood. It was the second year of
his occupation of the estate, and already he
had reared a very fair head of pheasants, for
he was an all-round sportsman, and as fond
of shooting with a shot-gun as with an eight-
bore rifle. We were three guns that day, Sir
Henry Curtis, old Quatermain, and myself, but
Sir Henry had to leave in the middle of the
afternoon in order to meet his agent and in-
spect an outlying farm where a new shed was

wanted. He was, however, coming back to dinner, and going to bring Captain Good with him, for Brayley Hall was not more than two miles from the Grange.

We had met with very fair sport, considering that we were only going through outlying covers for cocks. I think that we had killed twenty-seven, a woodcock, and a leash of partridges which we had got out of a driven covey. On our way home there lay a long narrow spinney which was very favorite "lie" for woodcock, and generally held a pheasant or two as well.

"Well, what do you say," said old Quatermain—"shall we beat through this for a finish?"

I assented, and he called to the keeper, who was following with a little knot of beaters, and told him to beat the spinney.

"Very well, sir," answered the man; "but it's getting wonderful dark, and the wind's rising a gale. It will take you all your time to hit a woodcock if the spinney holds one."

"You show us the woodcock, Jeffries," answered Quatermain, quickly, for he never liked being crossed in anything to do with sport, "and we will look after shooting them."

The man turned and went, rather sulkily. I heard him say to the under-keeper, "He's

pretty good the master is, I'm not saying he
isn't, but if he kills a woodcock in this light
and wind, I'm a Dutchman."

I think that Quatermain heard him too,
though he said nothing. The wind was rising
every minute, and by the time the beat began
it was blowing big guns. I stood at the right-
hand corner of the spinney, which curved round
somewhat, and Quatermain stood at the left,
some forty paces from me. Presently an old
cock-pheasant came rocketing over me, looking
as though the feathers were all being blown
out of his tail. I missed him clean with the
first barrel, and was never more pleased with
myself in my life than when I doubled him up
with the second, for the shot was not an easy
one. In the faint light I could just see Quatermain nodding his head in approval, when
through the groaning of the trees I heard
the shouts of the beaters. " Cock forward,
cock to the right." Then came a whole volley
of shouts : " Woodcock to the right," " Cock
to the left," " Cock over."

I looked up, and presently caught sight of
one of the woodcock coming down the wind
upon me like a flash. In that dim light I could
not follow all his movements as he zigzagged
through the naked tree-tops; indeed, I could

only see him when his wings flitted up. Now
he was passing me—*bang* and a flick of the
wing. I had missed him. *Bang* again. Surely he was down—no, there he went to my left.

"Cock to you," I shouted, stepping forward
so as to get Quatermain between me and the
faint angry light of the dying day, for I wanted
to see if he would "wipe my eye." I knew
him to be a wonderful shot, but that cock
would, I thought, puzzle him.

I saw him raise his gun ever so little and
bend forward, and at that moment out flashed
two woodcock into the open, the one I had
missed to his right, and the other to his left.
At the same time a fresh shout arose of,
"Woodcock over," and looking down the spinney I saw a third bird high up in the air, being
blown along like a brown and whirling leaf
straight over Quatermain's head. And then
followed the prettiest little bit of shooting that
I ever saw. The bird to the right was flying
low, not ten yards from the line of a hedge-
row, and Quatermain took him first because
he would become invisible the soonest of any.
Indeed, nobody who had not his hawk's eyes
could have seen to shoot him. But he saw
him well enough to kill him dead as a stone.
Then, turning sharply, he pulled on the second

bird at about forty-five yards, and over he went. By this time the third woodcock was nearly over him and flying very high, straight down the wind a hundred feet up or more, I should say. I saw him glance at it as he opened his gun, threw out the right cartridge and slipped in another, turning round as he did so. By this time the cock was nearly fifty yards away from him, and travelling like a flash. Lifting his gun, he fired after it, and, wonderful as the shot was, killed it dead. A tearing gust of wind caught the dead bird and blew it right away like a leaf torn from an oak, so that it fell a hundred and thirty yards off or more.

"I say, Quatermain," I said to him when the beaters were up, "do you often do this sort of thing?"

"Well," he answered, with a dry smile, "the last time I had to load three shots as quickly as that was at rather larger game. It was at elephants. I killed them all three as dead as I killed those woodcock; but it very nearly went the other way, I can tell you. I mean that they very nearly killed me."

Just at that moment the keeper came up. "Did you happen to get one of them there cocks, sir?" he said, with the air of a man who did not in the least expect an answer in the affirmative.

"Well, yes, Jeffries," answered Quatermain. "You will find one of them by the hedge, and another about fifty yards out by the plough there to the left."

The keeper had turned to go, looking a little astonished, when Quatermain called him back.

"Stop a bit, Jeffries," he said. "You see that pollard about one hundred and forty yards off? Well, there should be another woodcock down in a line with it, about sixty paces out in the field."

"Well, if that be'ant the very smartest bit of shooting," murmured Jeffries, and departed. After that we went home, and in due course Sir Henry Curtis and Captain Good turned up to dinner, the latter in the tightest and most ornamental dress suit I ever saw. I remember that the waistcoat was adorned with five pink coral buttons.

It was a very pleasant dinner. Old Quatermain was in excellent humor, induced, I think, by the recollection of his triumph over the doubting Jeffries. Good, too, was full of anecdotes. He told us a most miraculous story of how he once went shooting ibex in Kashmir.

These ibex, according to Good, he stalked early and late for four entire days. At last, on the morning of the fifth day, he succeeded in getting within range of the flock, which consisted of a magnificent old ram, with horns so long that I am afraid to mention their measure, and five or six females. Good crawled upon his stomach, painfully taking shelter behind rocks, . till he was within two hundred yards; then he drew a fine bead upon the old ram. At this moment, however, a diversion occurred. Some wandering native of the hills appeared upon a distant mountain-top. The females turned, and, rushing over a rock, vanished from Good's ken. But the old ram took a bolder course. In front of him stretched a mighty crevasse at least thirty feet in width. He went at it with a bound. While he was in mid-air Good fired, and killed him dead. The ram turned a complete somersault in space, and fell in such fashion that his horns hooked themselves upon a big projection of the opposite cliffs. There he hung, till Good, after a long and painful detour, gracefully dropped a lasso over him and fished him up.

This moving tale of wild adventure was received with undeserved incredulity.

" Well," said Good, " if you fellows won't

believe my story when I tell it—a perfectly
true story, mind—perhaps one of you will give
us a better; I'm not particular if it is true or
not." And he lapsed into a dignified silence.

"Now, Quatermain," I said, "don't let Good
beat you; let's hear how you killed those elephants you were talking about this evening
just after you shot the woodcocks."

"Well," said Quatermain, dryly, and with
something like a twinkle in his brown eyes,
"it is very hard fortune for a man to have to
follow on Good's 'spoor.' Indeed, if it were
not for that running giraffe, which, as you will
remember, Curtis, we saw Good bowl over
with a Martini rifle at three hundred yards,
I should almost have said that this was an
impossible tale."

Here Good looked up with an air of indig-
nant innocence.

"However," he went on, rising and lighting
his pipe, "if you fellows like, I will spin you
a yarn.

"I was telling one of you the other night
about those three lions, and how the lioness
finished my unfortunate 'voorlooper' Jim-
Jim, the boy whom we buried in the bread-
bag.

"Well, after that little experience I thought

that I would settle down a bit, so I went in for a venture with a man who, being of a speculative mind, had conceived the idea of running a store at Pretoria upon strictly cash principles. The arrangement was that I should find the capital, and he the experience. Our partnership was not of long duration. The Boers refused to pay cash, and at the end of four months my partner had the capital and I had the experience. After this I came to the conclusion that store-keeping was not in my line, and having four hundred pounds left, I sent my boy Harry to a school in Natal, and, buying an outfit with what remained of the money, started upon a big trip. This time I determined to go further afield than I had ever been before, so I got a passage for a few pounds in a trading brig that ran between Durband and Delagoa Bay. From Delagoa Bay I marched inland, accompanied by twenty porters, with the idea of striking up north towards the Limpopo, and keeping parallel to, but at a distance of about one hundred and fifty miles from, the coast. For the first twenty days of our journey we suffered a great deal from fever—that is, my men did, for I think that I am fever proof. Also I was hard put to it to keep the camp in meat, for

although the country proved to be very
sparsely populated, there was but little game
about. Indeed, during all that time I hardly
killed anything larger than a water-buck, and
water-buck is, as you know, not very appetiz-
ing food. On the twentieth day, however, we
came to the banks of a largish river, the Go-
nooroo it was called. This I crossed, and then
struck inland towards a great range of mountains, a continuation, as I believe, of the Dra-
kensberg range that skirts the coast of Natal,
the blue crests of which we could see lying on
the distant heavens like a shadow. From this
main range a great spur shot out some fifty
miles or so towards the coast, ending abruptly
in one tremendous peak. This spur I discovered separated the territories of two chiefs
named Nala and Wambe, Wambe's territory
being to the north and Nala's to the south.
Nala ruled a tribe of bastard Zulus called the
Butiana, and Wambe a much larger tribe called
the Matuku, which presented marked Basutu
characteristics. For instance, they had doors
and verandas to their huts, worked skins perfectly, and wore a waist-cloth, not a moocha.
The Butiana were more or less subject to the
Matuku, having been surprised by them some
twenty years before, and mercilessly slaugh-

tered down. The tribe was, however, now
recovering, and, as you may imagine, it did
not love the Matuku.

" Well, I heard as I went along that elephants
were very plentiful in the dense forests that lay
upon the slopes and at the foot of the mountains that bordered Wambe's territory. Also
I heard a very ill report of that worthy himself, who lived in a kraal upon the side of the
mountain, which was so strongly fortified as to
be practically impregnable. It was said that
he was the most cruel chief in this part of
Africa, and that he had murdered in cold
blood an entire party of English gentlemen
who, some seven years before, had gone into
his country to hunt elephants. They had an
old friend of mine with them as guide, John
Every by name, and often had I mourned over
his untimely death. All the same, Wambe or
no Wambe, I determined to hunt elephant in
his country. I never was afraid of natives,
and I was not going to show the white-feather
now. I am a bit of a fatalist, as you fellows
know, so I came to the conclusion that if it
was fated that Wambe should send me to join
my old friend Every, I should have to go and
there was an end of it. Meanwhile I meant
to hunt elephant with a peaceful heart.

"On the third day from the date of our sighting the great peak we found ourselves beneath its mighty shadow. Still following the course of the river which wound through the forests at the base of the peak, we entered the territory of the redoubtable Wambe. This, however, was not accomplished without a certain difference of opinion between my bearers and myself, for when we reached the spot where Wambe's boundary was supposed to run, the bearers sat down and emphatically refused to go a step farther. I sat down too, and argued with them, putting my fatalistic views before them as well as I was able. But I could not persuade them to look at the matter in the same light. 'At present,' they said, 'their skins were whole;' if they went into Wambe's country without his leave, they would soon be like a water-eaten leaf. It was very well for me to say that that would be Fate. Fate no doubt might be walking about in Wambe's country, but while they stopped outside they would not meet him.

"'Well,' I said to Gobo, my headman, 'and what do you mean to do?'

"'We mean to go back to the coast, Macumazahn,' he answered, insolently.

"'Do you?' I replied, for my bile was stirred.

' At any rate, Mr. Gobo, you and one or two others will never get there. See here, my friend,' and I took a repeating rifle and sat myself comfortably down, resting my back against a tree—' I have just breakfasted, and I had as soon spend the day here as anywhere else. Now if you or any of those men walk one step back from here and towards the coast I shall fire at you, and you know I don't miss.'

" The man fingered the spear he was carrying —luckily all the guns were stacked against the tree—and then turned as though to walk away, the others keeping their eyes 'fixed upon him all the while. I rose and covered him with the rifle, and though he kept up a brave appearance of unconcern, I saw that he was glancing nervously at me all the time. When he had gone about twenty yards, I spoke very quietly.

" ' Now, Gobo,' I said, ' come back, or I shall fire.'

" Of course this was taking a very high hand. I had no real right to kill Gobo or anybody else because they objected to running the risk of death by entering the territory of a hostile chief. But I felt that if I wished to keep up any authority it was absolutely necessary that I should push matters to the last extremity, short of actually shooting him.   And I stood there, looking as fierce as a lion, and keeping the sight of my rifle in a dead line for Gobo's ribs.   Then Gobo, feeling that the situation was getting strained, gave in.

"'Don't shoot, boss,' he shouted, throwing up his hand ; 'I will come with you.'

" 'I thought you would,' I answered, quietly. 'You see Fate walks outside Wambe's country as well as in it.'

" After that I had no more trouble, for Gobo was the ringleader, and when he collapsed the others collapsed also.   Harmony being thus restored, we crossed the line, and on the following morning I began shooting in good earnest.

CHAPTER II.

A MORNING'S SPORT.

"MOVING some five or six miles round the base
of the great peak of which I have spoken, we
came the same day to one of the fairest bits of
African country that I have seen outside of
Kukuanaland. At this spot the mountain spur
that runs out at right angles to the great range,
which stretches its mighty cloud-clad length
north and south as far as the eye can reach,
sweeps inward with a vast and splendid curve.
This curve measures some five-and-thirty miles
from point to point, and across its moonlike
segment the river flashed, a silver line of light.
On the farther side of the river is a measureless sea of swelling ground, a mighty natural
park covered with great patches of bush, some
of them being many square miles in extent,
which are separated one from another by
glades of grass land, broken here and there
with clumps of timber-trees, and in some in-
stances by curious isolated Koppies, and even

by single crags of granite, that start up into
the air as though they were monuments carved
by man, and not tombstones set by nature over
the grave of ages gone. On the west this beautiful plain is bordered by the lonely mountain
from the edge of which it rolls down towards
the feverish coast, but how far it runs to the
north I cannot say—eight days' journey, according to the natives, when it is lost in a
measureless swamp. On the hither side of the
river the scenery is different. Along the edge
of its banks, where the land is flat, are green
patches of swamp. Then comes a wide belt of
beautiful grass land, covered thick with game,
and sloping up very gently to the borders of
the forest, which, beginning at about a thousand feet above the level of the plain, clothes
the mountain-side almost to its crest. In this
forest grow great trees, most of them of the
yellow-wood species. Some of these trees are
so lofty that a bird in their top branches would
be out of range of an ordinary shot-gun. Another peculiar thing about them is that they
are, for the most part, covered with a dense
growth of the Ochella moss. Out of this moss
the natives manufacture a most excellent deep
purple dye, with which they stain tanned hides,
and also cloth when they happen to get any of

the latter. I do not think I ever saw anything more remarkable than the appearance of one of these mighty trees festooned from top to bottom with trailing wreaths of this sad-hued moss, in which the wind whispers gently as it stirs them. At a distance it looks like the gray locks of a Titan crowned with bright green leaves, and here and there starred with the rich bloom of orchids.

" The night of that day when I had my little difference of opinion with Gobo we camped upon the edge of this great forest, and on the following morning at daylight I started out shooting. As we were short of meat I determined to kill a buffalo, of which there were plenty about, before looking for traces of elephants. Not more than half a mile from camp we came across a trail like a cart-road, evidently made by a great herd of buffalo which had passed up at dawn from their feeding-ground in the marshes to spend the day in the cool air of the uplands. This trail I followed boldly, for such wind as there was blew straight down the mountain-side—that is, from the direction in which the buffalo had gone—to me. About a mile farther on the forest began to get dense, and the nature of the trail showed me that I must be close to my game.

Another two hundred yards, and the bush was so thick that had it not been for the trail we could scarcely have got through it. As it was, Gobo, who carried my eight-bore rifle (for I had the .570 express in my hand), and the other two men whom I had taken with me, showed the very strongest dislike to going any farther, pointing out that there was 'no room to run away.' I told them that they need not come unless they liked, but that I was certainly going on, and then, growing ashamed, they came. Another fifty yards, and the trail opened into a little glade. I knelt down and peeped and peered, but no buffalo could I see. Evidently the herd had broken up here — I knew that from the spoor—and penetrated the opposite bush in little troops. I crossed the glade, and choosing one line of spoor, followed it for some sixty yards, when it became clear to me that I was surrounded by buffalo, and yet so dense was the cover that I could not see one. A few yards to my left I could hear one rubbing its horns against a tree, while from my right came an occasional low throaty grunt which told me that I was uncomfortably near an old bull. I crept on towards him with my heart in my mouth, as gently as though I were walking upon eggs for a bet, lifting every little

bit of wood in my path and placing it behind
me, lest it should crack and warn the game.
Behind me in single file came my three retainers, and I don't know which of them looked
the most frightened. Presently Gobo touched
my leg. I looked round, and saw him pointing
slantwise towards the left. I lifted my head a
little and peeped over a mass of creepers. Beyond the creepers was a dense bush of sharp-
pointed aloes, of that kind of which the leaves
project laterally, and on the other side of the
aloes, not fifteen paces from us, I made out the
horns, neck, and the ridge of the back of a
tremendous old bull. I took my eight-bore,
and getting on to my knee, prepared to shoot
him through the neck, taking my chance of
cutting his spine. I had already covered him
as well as the aloe leaves would allow, when
he gave a kind of sigh and lay down.

"I looked round in dismay. What was to be
done now? I could not see to shoot him lying
down, even if my bullet would have pierced
the intervening aloes, which was doubtful, and
if I stood up he would either run away or
charge me. I reflected, and came to the conclusion that the only thing to do was to lie
down also, for I did not fancy wandering after
other buffalo in that dense bush. If a buffalo

lies down, it is clear that he must get up again
some time; so it was only a case of patience—
'fighting the fight of sit down,' as the Zulus
say.

"Accordingly I sat down and lighted a pipe,
thinking that the smell of it might reach the
buffalo and make him get up. But the wind
was the wrong way, and it did not, so when
it was done I lit another. Afterwards I had
cause to regret that pipe.

"Well, we squatted like this for between half·
and three quarters of an hour, till at last I began to grow heartily sick of the performance.
It was about as dull a business as the last hour
of a comic opera. I could hear buffalo snorting and moving all round, and see the red-
beaked tic birds flying off their backs with a
kind of hiss something like that of an English
misselthrush, but I could not see a single buffalo. As for my old bull, I think he must have
slept the sleep of the just, for he never even
stirred. Just as I was making up my mind
that something must be done to save the situation, my attention was attracted by a curious
grinding noise. At first I thought that it must
be a buffalo chewing the cud, but was obliged
to abandon the idea because the noise was
too loud. I shifted myself round and stared

through the cracks in the bush in the direction
whence the sound seemed to come, and once
I thought that I saw something gray moving
about fifty yards off, but could not make certain. Although the grinding noise still continued, I could see nothing more, so I gave up
thinking about it, and once again turned my
attention to the buffalo. Presently, however,
something happened. Suddenly from about
forty yards away there came a tremendous
snorting sound, more like that made by an
engine getting a heavy train under way than
anything else in the world.

" 'By Jove!' I thought, turning round in the
direction from which the grinding sound had
come, 'that must be a rhinoceros, and he has
got our wind.' For, as you fellows know,
there is no mistaking the sound made by a
rhinoceros when he gets wind of you.

" Another second and there was a most tremendous crashing noise. Before I could think
what to do, before I could even get up, the
bush behind me seemed to burst asunder, and
there appeared, not eight yards from us, the
great horn and wicked twinkling eye of a huge
charging rhinoceros. He had winded us or
my pipe, I do not know which, and, after the
fashion of these brutes, had charged up the

scent. I could not rise, I could not even get
the gun up—I had no time. All that I was
able to do was to roll over as far out of the
monster's path as the bush would allow. Another second and he was over me, his great
bulk towering above me like a mountain, and,
upon my word, I could not get his smell out
of my nostrils for a week. Circumstances im-
pressed it on my memory, at least I suppose
so. His hot breath blew upon my face, one
of his front feet just missed my head, and his
hind one actually trod upon the loose part of
my trouser and pinched a little bit of my skin.
I saw him pass over me, lying as I was upon
my back, and next second I saw something
else. My men were a little behind me, and
therefore straight in the path of the rhinoceros.
One of them flung himself backward into the
bush, and thus avoided him. The second, with
a wild yell, sprang to his feet and bounded like
an India-rubber ball right into the aloe bush,
landing well among the spikes. But the third
—it was my friend Gobo—could not by any
means get away. He managed to gain his feet
and that was all. The rhinoceros was charging
with his head low. His great horn passed between Gobo's legs, and feeling something on
his nose, he jerked it up. Away went Gobo

high into the air. He turned a complete somersault at the apex of the curve, and as he did so
I caught sight of his face. It was gray with
terror, and his mouth was wide open. Down
he came, right on to the great brute's rump,
and that broke his fall. But luckily for him,
the rhinoceros never turned. He crashed
straight through the aloe bush, only missing
the man who had jumped into it by about a
yard. Then followed a complication. The
sleeping buffalo on the farther side of the bush,
hearing the noise, sprang to his feet, and for a
second, not knowing what to do, stood still.
At that instant the huge rhinoceros blundered
right on to him, and getting his horn beneath
his stomach, gave him such a fearful dig that
the buffalo was turned over on to his back, while
his assailant went a most amazing cropper over
his carcass. In another moment, however, he
was up, and, wheeling round to the left, crashed
through the bush down-hill towards the open
country.

"Instantly the whole place became alive with
alarming sounds. In every direction troops of
snorting buffalo charged through the forest,
wild with fright, while the injured bull on the
farther side of the bush began to bellow like a
mad thing. I lay quite still for a moment, de-

voutly praying that none of the flying buffalo
would come my way. Then when the danger
lessened I got on to my feet, shook myself, and
looked round. One of my boys, he who had
thrown himself backward into the bush, was
already half-way up a tree; if heaven had been
at the top of it he could not have climbed
quicker. Gobo was lying close to me, groaning vigorously, but, as I suspected, quite unhurt; while from the aloe bush into which
Number Three had bounded like a tennis-ball,
came a succession of the most piercing yells.
I looked, and saw that the unfortunate fellow was in a very tight place. A great spike
of aloe had run through the back of his skin
waist-belt, though without piercing his flesh,
in such a fashion that it was impossible for
him to move, while within six feet of him the
injured buffalo bull, thinking, no doubt, that
he was the aggressor, bellowed and ramped to
get at him, tearing at the thick aloes with his
great horns. That no time was to be lost if I
wished to save the man's life was very clear.
So seizing my eight-bore, which was fortunately uninjured, I took a pace to the left, for the
rhinoceros had enlarged the hole in the bush,
and aimed at the point of the buffalo's shoulder, for on account of the position I could not

get a fair side shot for the heart. As I did so
I saw that the rhinoceros had given the bull a
tremendous wound in the stomach, and that
the shock of the encounter had put his left
hind-leg out of joint at the hip. I fired, and
the bullet, striking the shoulder, broke it, and
knocked the buffalo down. I knew that he
could not get up any more, because he was
now injured fore and aft, so, notwithstanding
his terrific bellows, I scrambled round to where
he was. There he lay, glaring furiously and
tearing up the soil with his horns. Stepping
up to within two yards of him, I aimed at the
vertebra of his neck, and fired. The bullet
struck true, and with a thud he dropped his
great head upon the ground, groaned and died.

"This little matter having been attended to,
I, with the assistance of Gobo, who had now
found his feet, went on to extricate the unfortunate companion from the aloe bush. This we
found a thorny task, but at last he was dragged
forth uninjured, though in a very pious and
prayerful frame of mind. His 'spirit had
certainly looked that way,' he said, or he
would now have been dead. As I never like
to interfere with true piety, I did not venture
to suggest that his spirit had deigned to make
use of my eight-bore in his interest.

" Having despatched this boy back to the
camp to tell the bearers to come and cut that
buffalo up, I bethought me that I owed that
rhinoceros a grudge which I should love to re-
pay. So without saying a word of what was
in my mind to Gobo, who was now more than
ever convinced that Fate walked about loose
in Wambe's country, I just followed on his
spoor. He had crashed through the bush till
he reached the little glade. Then moderating
his pace somewhat, he had followed the glade
down its entire length and once more turned
to the right, through the forest, shaping his
course for the open land that lies between the
edge of the bush and the river. Having followed him for a mile or so farther, I found
myself quite on the open. I took out my
glasses and searched the plain. About a mile
ahead was something brown—as I thought,
the rhinoceros ; I advanced another quarter of
a mile and looked once more—it was not the
rhinoceros, but a big ant-heap. This was puz-
zling, but I did not like to give it up, because
I knew from his spoor that he must be somewhere ahead. But as the wind was blowing
straight from me towards the line that he had
followed, and as a rhinoceros can smell you for
about a mile, it would not, I felt, be safe to fol-

low his spoor any farther. So I made a detour of a mile or more, till I was nearly opposite the ant-heap, and then once more searched
the plain. It was no good; I could see nothing of him, and was about to give it up and
start after some oryx I saw in the distance,
when suddenly, at a distance of about three
hundred yards from the ant-heap, and on its
farther side, I saw my rhino stand up in a
patch of grass.

"'Heavens!' I thought to myself, 'he's off
again.' But no; after standing staring for a
minute or two, he once more lay down.

"Now I found myself in a quandary. As
you know, a rhinoceros is a very short-sighted
brute; indeed, his sight is as bad as his scent
is good. Of this fact he is perfectly aware,
but he always makes the most of his natural
gifts. For instance, when he lies down he in-
variably does so with his head down wind.
Thus if any enemy crosses his wind, he will
still be able to escape or attack him, and if,
on the other hand, the danger approaches up
wind, he will at least have a chance of seeing
it. Otherwise one might, by walking delicately, actually kick him up like a partridge if only
the advance was made up wind.

"Well, the point was how on earth should

I get within shot of this rhinoceros. After much deliberation I determined to try a side advance, thinking that I might so get a shoulder-shot. Accordingly we started in a crouching attitude, I first, Gobo holding on to my coat-tails, and the other boy on to Gobo's moocha. I always adopt this plan when stalking big game, for if you follow any other system the bearers will get out of line. We got to within three hundred yards right enough, and then the real difficulties began. The grass had been so closely eaten off by game that there was scarcely any cover. Consequently it was necessary to go on to our hands and knees, which in my case involved laying down the eight-bore at every step and then lifting it up again. However, I wriggled along somehow, and if it had not been for Gobo and his friend, no doubt everything would have gone well. But as you have, I dare say, observed, a native out stalking is always of that mind which is supposed to actuate an ostrich. So long as his head is hidden he seems to think that nothing else can be seen. So it was in this instance: Gobo and the other boy crept along on their hands and toes with their heads well down, but, though unfortunately I did not notice it till too late, bearing the fundamental portions

of their frames high in the air. Now all animals are quite as suspicious of this end of man-
kind as they are of his face, and of this fact I
soon had a proof. Just when we had got within
about two hundred yards, and I was congratulating myself that I had not had this long
crawl, with the sun beating on the back of my
neck like a furnace, all for nothing, I heard the
hissing notes of the rhinoceros-birds, and up
flew four or five of them from the brute's
back, where they had been comfortably em-
ployed in catching tics. Now this performance on the part of the birds is to a rhinoceros
what the word "cave" is to a schoolboy; it
puts him on the *qui vive* at once. Before the
birds were well in the air I saw the grass stir.

"'Down you go!' I whispered to the boys,
and as I did so the rhinoceros got up and
glared suspiciously around. But he could see
nothing; indeed, if we had been standing up I
doubt if he would have seen us at that distance. So he merely gave two or three sniffs,
and then lay down, his head still down wind,
the birds once more settling on his back.

"But it was clear to me that he was sleeping
with one eye open, and generally in a suspicious and unchristian frame of mind, and that
it was useless to proceed farther on that stalk;

so we quietly withdrew to consider the position
and study the ground. The results were not
satisfactory. There was absolutely no cover
about except the ant-heap, which was some
three hundred yards from the rhinoceros upon
his up-wind side. I knew that if I tried to
stalk him in front I should fail, and so I should
if I attempted to do so from the farther side;
he or the birds would see me. So I came to a
conclusion: I would go to the ant-heap, which
would give him my wind, and instead of stalking him I would let him stalk me. It was a
bold step, and one which I should never advise
a hunter to take, but somehow I felt as though
Rhino and I must play the hand out.

"I explained my intentions to the men, who
both held up their hands in horror. Their
fears for my safety were a little mitigated,
however, when I told them that I did not expect them to come with me.

"Gobo breathed a prayer that I might not
meet Fate walking about, and the other one
sincerely trusted that my spirit might look my
way when the rhinoceros charged, and then
they both departed to a place of safety.

"Taking my eight-bore and half a dozen
spare cartridges in my pocket, I made a detour,
and, reaching the ant-heap in safety, lay down.

For a moment the wind had dropped, but
presently a gentle puff of air passed over me
and blew on towards the rhinoceros. By the
way, I wonder what it is that smells so strong
about a man. Is it his body or his breath? I
have never been able to make out, but I saw
somewhere the other day that in the duck de-
coys the man who is working the ducks holds
a little piece of burning turf before his mouth,
and that if he does this they cannot smell
him, which looks as though it were the breath.
Well, whatever it was about me that attracted
his attention, the rhinoceros soon smelt me, and
within half a minute after the puff of wind had
passed he was up and turning round to get his
head up wind. There he stood for a few seconds and sniffed, and then he began to move,
first of all at a trot, then, as the scent grew
stronger, at a furious gallop. On he came,
snorting like a runaway engine, with his tail
stuck straight up in the air; if he had seen me
lie down there he could not have made a better
line. It was rather nervous work, I can tell
you, lying there waiting for his onslaught, for
he looked like a mountain of flesh. I determined, however, not to fire till I could plainly
see his eye, for I think that rule always gives
one the right distance for big game. So I

rested my rifle on the ant-heap and waited for
him, kneeling. At last, when he was about
forty yards away, I saw that the time had
come, and aiming straight for the middle of
the chest, I pulled.

"*Thud* went the heavy bullet, and with a
tremendous snort over rolled the rhinoceros beneath its shock, just like a shot rabbit. But
if I had thought that he was done for I was
mistaken, for in another second he was up and
coming at me as hard as ever, only with his
head held low. I waited till he was within
ten yards, in the hope that he would expose
his chest, but he would do nothing of the sort.
So I just had to fire at his head with the left
barrel, and take my chance. Well, as luck
would have it, of course the animal put its
horn in the way of the bullet, which cut clean
through it about three inches above the root,
and then glanced off into space. After that
things got rather serious. My gun was empty,
and the rhinoceros was rapidly arriving—so
rapidly, indeed, that I came to the conclusion
that I had better make way for him. Accordingly I jumped to my feet and ran to the right
as hard as I could go. As I did so, he arrived
full tilt, knocked my friendly ant-heap flat, and
for the second time that day went a most mag-

nificent cropper. This gave me a few seconds'
start, and I ran down wind—my word, I did
run. Unfortunately, however, my modest retreat was observed, and the rhinoceros, as soon
as he got his legs again, set to work to run after me. Now no man on earth can run as fast
as an irritated rhinoceros can gallop, and I
knew that he must soon catch me up. But
having some slight experience of this sort of
thing, I, luckily for myself, kept my head, and
as I fled I managed to open my rifle, get the
old cartridges out, and put two fresh ones in.
To do this I had to steady my pace a little,
and by the time that I had snapped the rifle
to, I heard him snorting and thundering away
within a few paces of my back. I stopped,
and as I did so rapidly cocked the rifle, and
slewed round upon my heel. By this time the
brute was within six or seven yards of me, but
luckily his head was up. I lifted the rifle and
fired at him. It was a snap shot, but the bullet struck him in the chest within three inches
of the first, and found its way into his lungs.
It did not stop him, however, so all I could do
was to bound to one side, which I did with
surprising activity, and as he brushed past me
fire the other barrel into his side. That did
for him. The ball passed in behind the shoul-

der and right through his heart. He fell over
on to his side, gave one most awful squeal—a
dozen pigs could not have made such a noise—
and promptly died, keeping his wicked eyes
wide open all the time.

"As for me, I blew my nose, and going up
to the rhinoceros, sat on his head, and reflected
that I had had a capital morning's shooting.

CHAPTER III.

"AFTER this, as it was now mid-day, and 1
had killed enough meat, we marched back
triumphantly to camp, where I proceeded to
concoct a stew of buffalo beef and compressed
vegetables. When this was done we ate the
stew, and then I had a nap. About four o'clock,
however, Gobo woke me up, and told me that
the headman of one of Wambe's kraals had arrived to see me. I ordered him to be brought
up, and presently he came, a little, wizened,
talkative old man, with a waist-cloth round
his middle, and a greasy, frayed kaross made
of the skins of rock rabbits over his shoulders.

"I told him to sit down, and then abused him
roundly. 'What did he mean,' I asked, 'by
disturbing me in this rude way? How did he
dare to cause a person of my quality and evi-
dent importance to be awakened in order to
interview his entirely contemptible self?'

"I spoke thus because I knew that it would

produce an impression on him. Nobody except a really great man, he would argue, would
dare to speak to him in that fashion. Most
savages are desperate bullies at heart, and
look on insolence as a sign of power.

" The old man instantly collapsed. He was
utterly overcome, he said ; his heart was split
in two, and well realized the extent of his mis-
behavior. But the occasion was very urgent.
He heard that a mighty hunter was in the
neighborhood, a beautiful white man — how
beautiful he could not have imagined had he
not seen—(this to me!), and he came to beg
his assistance. The truth was that three bull
elephants such as no man ever saw had for
years been the terror of their kraal, which was
but a small place, a cattle kraal of the great
chief Wambe's, where they lived to keep the
cattle. And now, of late, these elephants had
done them much damage, but last night they
had destroyed a whole patch of mealie land,
and he feared that if they came back they
would all starve next season for want of food.
Would the mighty white man then be pleased
to come and kill the elephants ? It would be
easy for him to do; oh, most easy ! It was
only necessary that he should hide himself in
a tree, for there was a full moon, and then

when the elephants appeared he would speak
to them with the gun, and they would fall
down dead, and there would be an end of their
troubling.

"Of course I hemmed and hawed, and made
a great favor of consenting to this proposal,
though really I was delighted to have such a
chance. One of the conditions that I made
was that a messenger should at once be despatched to Wambe, whose kraal was two days'
journey from where I was, telling him that I
proposed to come and pay my respects to him
in a few days, and to ask his formal permis-
sion to shoot in his country. Also, I intimated
that I was prepared to present him with 'hongo,' that is, blackmail, and that I hoped to
do a little trade with him in ivory, of which
I heard he had a great quantity. This message the old gentleman promised to despatch
at once, though there was something about his
manner which showed me that he was doubtful as to how it would be received. After that
we struck our camp, and moved on to the
kraal, which we reached about an hour before
sunset. This kraal was a collection of huts
surrounded by a slight thorn fence; perhaps
there were ten of them in all. It was situated
in a kloof of the mountain, with a rivulet flow-

ing down it. The kloof was densely wooded,
but for some distance above the kraal it was
free from bush, and here, on the rich deep
ground brought down by the rivulet were the
cultivated lands, in extent somewhere about
twenty or twenty-five acres. On the kraal
side of these lands stood a single hut which
served for mealie stores, which at the moment
was used as a dwelling-place by an old woman,
the first wife of our friend the headman.

"It appears that this old lady, having had
some difference of opinion with her husband
about the extent of authority allowed to a
younger and more amiable wife, had refused
to dwell in the kraal any more, and, by way
of marking her displeasure, had taken up her
abode among the mealies. As the issue will
show, she was, as it happened, cutting off her
nose to spite her face.

"Close by this hut grew a large banyan-tree.
A glance at the mealie grounds showed me
that the old headman had not exaggerated the
mischief done by the elephants to his crops,
which were now getting ripe. Nearly half of
the entire patch was destroyed. The great
brutes had eaten all they could, and the rest
they had trampled down. I went up to their
spoor, and started back in amazement. Never

had I seen such spoor before. It was simply enormous, more especially that of one old bull, that had, so said the natives, but a single tusk. One might have used any of the footprints for a hip bath.

"Having taken stock of the position, my next step was to make arrangements for the fray. The three bulls, according to the natives, had been spoored into the dense patch of bush above the kloof. Now it seemed to me very probable that they would return to-night to feed on the remainder of the ripening mealies. If so, there was a bright moon, and it struck me that by the exercise of a little ingenuity I might bag one or more of them without exposing myself to any risk, which, having the highest respect for the aggressive powers of bull elephants, was a great consideration to me. This, then, was my plan: To the right of the huts as you look up the kloof, and commanding the mealie lands, stands the banyantree that I have mentioned. Into that banyantree I made up my mind to go. Then if the elephants appeared I should get a shot at them. I announced my intentions to the headman of the kraal, who was delighted. 'Now,' he said, 'his people might sleep in peace, for while the mighty white hunter sat aloft like

a spirit watching over the welfare of his kraal
what was there to fear ?'

"I told him that he was an ungrateful brute
to think of sleeping in peace while I, perched
like a wounded vulture on a tree, watched for
his welfare in wakeful sorrow, and once more
he collapsed, and owned that my words were
' sharp but just.'

"However, as I have said, confidence was com-
pletely restored, and that evening everybody
in the kraal, including the superannuated victim of jealousy in the little hut where the mealie cobs were stored, went to bed with a sense
of sweet security from elephants and all other
animals that prowl by night.

"For my part, I pitched my camp below the
kraal; and then having procured a beam of
wood from the headman—rather a rotten one,
by the way—I set it across two boughs that
ran out laterally from the banyan-tree at a
height of about twenty-five feet from the
ground, in such fashion that I and another
man could sit upon it with our legs hanging
down, and rest ourselves with our backs against
the bole of the tree. This done, I went back
to the camp and had my supper. About nine
o'clock, half an hour before the moonrise, I
summoned Gobo—who, thinking that he had

had about enough of the delights of big-game hunting for that day, did not altogether relish the job—and despite his remonstrances, gave him my eight-bore to carry, I having the .570 express, and set out for the tree. It was very dark, but we found it without difficulty, though climbing it was a more complicated matter. However, at last we got up, and sat down like two little boys on a form that is too high for them, and waited. I did not dare to smoke, because I remembered the rhinoceros, and feared that the elephants might wind the tobacco if they should come my way, and this made the business more wearisome. So I fell to thinking, and wondering at the vastness of the silence.

"At last the moon came up, and with it a moaning wind, at the breath of which the silence began to whisper mysteriously. Lonely enough, in the new-born light, looked the wide expanse of mountain, plain, and forest, more like some twilight vision of a dream, some faint reflection from a fair world of peace beyond our ken, than the mere face of garish earth made silvery soft with sleep. Indeed, had it not been for the fact that I was beginning to find the log on which I sat very hard, I should have grown quite sentimental over

the beautiful sight. But I will defy anybody
to become sentimental when seated in the damp
on a very rough beam of wood half-way up a
tree. So I merely made a mental note that it
was a particularly lovely night, and turned my
attention to the prospect of elephants. But
no elephants came, and after waiting for another hour or so, I think that what between
weariness and disgust I must have dropped
into a gentle doze. Presently I awoke with a
start. Gobo, who was perched close to me,
but as far off as the beam would allow—for
neither white man nor black like the aroma
which each vows is the peculiar and disa-
greeable property of the other—was faintly,
very faintly, clicking his forefinger against his
thumb. I knew by this signal, a very favorite one among native hunters and gun-bearers,
that he must have seen or heard something.
I looked at his face, and saw that he was staring excitedly towards the dim edge of the bush
beyond the deep green line of mealies. I stared
too, and listened. Presently I heard a soft
large sound, as though a giant were gently
stretching out his hands and pressing back the
ears of standing corn. Then came a pause,
and then out into the open majestically stalked
the largest elephant I ever saw or ever shall

see. Heavens! what a monster he was! and how the moonlight gleamed upon his one splendid tusk—for the other was missing—as he stood among the mealies, gently moving his enormous ears to and fro, and testing the wind with his trunk! While I was still marvelling at his girth, and speculating upon the weight of that huge tusk, which I swore should be my tusk before very long, out stepped a second bull and stood beside him. He was not quite so tall, but he seemed to me to be almost thicker-set than the first, and even in that light I could see that both his tusks were perfect. Another pause, and the third emerged. He was shorter than either of the others, but higher in the shoulder than No. 2, and when I tell you that, as I afterwards learned from actual measurement, the smallest of these three mighty bulls measured twelve feet one and a half inches at the shoulder, it will give you some idea of their size. The three formed into line, and stood still for a minute, the one-tusked bull gently caressing the elephant on the left with his trunk.

"Then they began to feed, walking forward and slightly to the right as they gathered great bunches of the sweet mealies and thrust them into their mouths. All this time they were

more than a hundred and twenty yards away
from me (this I knew because I had paced the
distances from the tree to various points), much
too far to allow of my attempting a shot at
them in that uncertain light. They fed in a
semicircle, gradually drawing round towards
the hut, near my tree, in which the corn was
stored and the old woman slept.

" This went on for between an hour and an
hour and a half, till what between excitement
and hope that maketh the heart sick I got so
weary that I was actually contemplating a descent from the tree and a moonlight stalk.
Such an act in ground so open would have been
that of a stark staring lunatic, and that I
should even have been contemplating it will
show you the condition of my mind. But
everything comes to him who knows how to
wait, and sometimes too to him who doesn't,
and so at last those elephants, or rather one of
them, came to me. After they had fed their
fill, which was a very large one, the noble three
stood once more in line some seventy yards to
the left of the hut and in the edge of the cultivated lands, or in all about eighty-five yards
from where I was perched. Then at last the
one with the single tusk made a peculiar rat-
tling noise in his trunk, just as though he were

blowing his nose, and without more ado began
to walk deliberately towards the hut where
the old woman slept. I got my rifle ready,
and glanced up at the moon, only to discover
that a new complication was looming in the
immediate future. I have said that a wind
rose with the moon. Well, the wind brought
rain-clouds along its track. Several light ones
had already for a little while lessened the light,
though without obscuring it, and now two
more were coming rapidly up, both of them
very black and dense. The first cloud was
small and long, and the one behind big and
broad. I remember noticing that the pair of
them bore a most comical resemblance to a
dray drawn by a very long raw-boned horse.
As luck would have it, just as the elephant got
within twenty-five yards or so of me, the head
of the horse-cloud floated over the face of the
moon, rendering it impossible for me to fire.
In the faint twilight which remained, however,
I could just make out the gray mass of the
great brute still advancing towards the hut.
Then the light went altogether, and I had to
trust to my ears. I heard him fumbling with
his trunk, apparently at the roof of the hut.
Next came a sound as of straw being drawn
out, and then for a little while there was com-

plete silence. The cloud began to pass. I
could see the outline of the elephant; he was
standing with his head right over the top of
the hut. But I could not see his trunk, and
no wonder, for it was *inside the hut*. He had
thrust it right through the roof, and attracted,
no doubt, by the smell of the mealies, was grop-
ing about with it inside. It was growing light
now, and I got my rifle ready, when suddenly
there was a most awful yell, and I saw the
trunk reappear, and in its mighty fold the old
woman who had been sleeping in the hut. Out
she came through the hole like a periwinkle
on the point of a pin, still wrapped up in her
blanket, and her skinny legs and arms stretched
to the four points of the compass, and, as she
did so, gave that most alarming screech. I
really don't know who was the most frightened, she or I or the elephant. At any rate,
the last was considerably startled; he had been
fishing for mealies—the old woman was a mere
accident, and one that greatly discomposed his
nerves. He gave a sort of trumpet, and threw
her away from him right in the crown of a low
mimosa-tree, where she stuck shrieking like a
metropolitan engine. The old bull lifted his
tail, and, flapping his great ears, prepared for
flight. I put up my eight-bore, and, aiming

hastily at the point of his shoulder (for he was broadside on), I fired. The report rang out like thunder, making a thousand echoes in the quiet hills. I saw him go down all of a heap, as though he were stone-dead. Then, alas! whether it was the kick of the heavy rifle or the excited bump of that idiot Gobo, or both together, or merely an unhappy coincidence, I do not know, but the rotten beam broke, and I went down too, landing flat at the foot of the tree upon a certain humble portion of the human frame. The shock was so severe that I felt as though all my teeth were flying through the roof of my mouth; but although I sat slightly stunned for a few seconds, luckily for me I fell light, and was not in any way injured. Meanwhile the elephant began to scream with fear and fury, and, attracted by his cries, the other two came charging up. I felt for my rifle; it was not there. Then I remembered that I had rested it on a fork of the bough in order to fire, and doubtless there it remained. My position now was very unpleasant. I did not dare to try and climb the tree again, which, shaken as I was, would have been a task of some difficulty, because the elephants would certainly see me, and Gobo, who had clung to a bough, was still aloft with the other rifle. I

could not run, because there was no shelter
near.   Under these circumstances I did the
only thing feasible—clambered round the trunk
as softly as possible, and, keeping one eye on
the elephants, whispered to Gobo to bring
down the rifle, and awaited the development
of the situation.   I knew that if the elephants
did not see me, which, luckily, they were too
engaged to do, they would not smell me, for I
was up wind.   Gobo, however, either did not,
or, preferring the safety of the tree, would not,
hear me.   He said the former, but I believed
the latter, for I knew that he was not enough
of a sportsman to really enjoy shooting elephants by moonlight in the open.   So there I
was behind my tree, dismayed, unarmed, but
highly interested, for I was witnessing a remarkable performance.

   "When the two other bulls arrived the
wounded elephant on the ground ceased to
scream, but began to make a low moaning
noise and gently touch the wound near his
shoulder, from which the blood was literally
spouting out. The other two seemed to under-
stand; at any rate, they did this: Kneeling
down on either side, they got their trunks and
tusks underneath him, and, aided by his own
efforts, with one great lift got him on his feet.

Then, leaning against him on either side to support him, they marched off at a walk in the direction of the village.* It was a pitiful sight, and even then it made me feel a brute.

"Presently from a walk, as the wounded elephant gathered himself together a little, they broke into a trot, and after that I could follow them no longer with my eyes, for the second black cloud came up over the moon and put her out as an extinguisher puts out a dip. I say with my eyes, but my ears still gave me a very fair notion of what was going on. When the cloud came up the three terrified animals were heading directly for the kraal, probably because the way was open and the path easy. I fancy that they got confused in the darkness, for when they came to the kraal fence they did not turn aside, but crashed through it. Then there were 'times,' as the Irish servant-girl says in the American book. Having taken the fence, they thought that they might as well take the huts also, so they just ran right over them. One hive-shaped hut

---

* The Editor would have been inclined to think that in relating this incident Mr. Quatermain was making himself interesting at the expense of the exact truth, did it not happen that a similar incident has come within his own knowledge.—ED.

was turned straight over on to its top, and
when I arrived on the scene the people who
had been sleeping there were bumbling about
inside like bees disturbed at night, while two
more were crushed flat, and a third had all its
side torn out. Oddly enough, however, nobody
was hurt, though several people had a narrow
escape of being trodden to death.

" On arrival I found the old headman in a
state painfully like that favored by Greek art,
dancing about in front of his ruined abodes as
vigorously as though he had just been stung
by a scorpion.

" I asked him what ailed him, and he burst
out into a flood of abuse. He called me a wiz-
ard, a sham, a fraud, a bringer of bad luck. I
had promised to kill the elephants, and I had so
arranged things that the elephants had nearly
killed him, etc.

" This, still smarting, or rather aching, as I
was from that most terrific bump, was too
much for my feelings, so I just made a rush
at my friend, and, getting him by the ear, I
banged his head against the doorway of his
own hut, which was all there was left of it.

" ' You wicked old scoundrel,' I said, ' you
dare to complain about your own trifling in-
conveniences, when you gave me a rotten beam

to sit on, and thereby delivered me to the
fury of the elephant' (*bump! bump! bump!*),
'when your own wife' (*bump!*) 'has just
been dragged out of her hut' (*bump!*) 'like
a snail from its shell and thrown by the Earth-
shaker into a tree' (*bump! bump!*).

"'Mercy, my father, mercy!' gasped the old
fellow. 'Truly I have done amiss—my heart
tells me so.'

"'I should hope it did, you old villain'
(*bump!*).

"'Mercy, great white man. I thought the
log was sound. But what says the unequalled
chief—is the old woman, my wife, indeed dead?
Ah, if she is dead all may yet prove to have
been for the very best;' and he clasped his
hands and looked up piously to heaven, in which
the moon was once more shining brightly.

"I let go his ear and burst out laughing, the
whole scene and his devout aspirations for the
decease of the partner of his joys, or rather
woes, were so intensely ridiculous.

"'No, you old iniquity,' I answered; 'I left
her in the top of a thorn-tree, screaming like
a thousand bluejays. The elephant put her
there.'

"'Alas! alas!' he said, 'surely the back of
the ox is shaped to the burden. Doubtless,

my father, she will come down when she is
tired ;' and without troubling himself further
about the matter, he began to blow at the
smouldering embers of the fire.

"And, as a matter of fact, she did appear a
few minutes later, considerably scratched and
startled, but none the worse.

"After that I made my way to my little
camp, which, fortunately, the elephants had
not walked over, and wrapping myself up in
a blanket, was soon fast asleep.

"And so ended my first round with those
three elephants.

CHAPTER IV.

THE LAST ROUND.

" On the morrow I woke up full of painful recollections, and not without a certain feeling of gratitude to the Powers above that I was there to wake up. Yesterday had been a tempestuous day ; indeed, what between buffalo, rhinoceros, and elephant, it had been very tempestuous. Having realized this fact, I next bethought me of those magnificent tusks, and instantly, early as it was, broke the tenth commandment. I coveted my neighbor's tusks, if an elephant could be said to be my neighbor *de jure*, as certainly, so recently as the previous night, he had been *de facto*—a much closer neighbor than I cared for, indeed. Now when you covet your neighbor's goods, the best thing, if not the most moral thing, to do is to enter his house as a strong man armed, and take them. I was not a strong man, but, having recovered my eight-bore, I was armed, and so was the other strong man, the elephant with

the tusks. Consequently I prepared for a struggle to the death. In other words, I summoned
my faithful retainers, and told them that I was
now going to follow those elephants over the
edge of the world, if necessary. They showed
a certain bashfulness about the business, but
they did not gainsay me, because they dared
not. Ever since I had prepared with all due
solemnity to execute the rebellious Gobo they
had conceived a great respect for me.

"So I went up to bid adieu to the old headman, whom I found alternately contemplating the ruins of his kraal and, with the able
assistance of his last wife, thrashing the jeal-
ous lady who had slept in the mealie hut, because she was, as he declared, the author of
all his sorrows.

"Leaving them to work a way through their
domestic differences, I levied a supply of vege-
table food from the kraal in consideration of
services rendered, and left them with my bless-
ing. I do not know how they settled matters,
because I have not seen them since.

"Then I started on the spoor of the three
bulls. For a couple of miles or so below the
kraal, as far, indeed, as the belt of swamp that
bordered the river, the ground was at this spot
rather stony, and clothed with scattered bushes.

Rain had fallen towards the daybreak, and this fact, together with the nature of the soil, made spooring a very difficult business. The wounded bull had indeed bled freely, but the rain had washed the blood off the leaves and grass, and the ground, being so rough and hard, had not taken the footmarks so clearly as was convenient. However, we got along, though slowly, partly by the spoor, and partly by carefully lifting leaves and blades of grass, and finding blood enough underneath them, for the blood gushing from a wounded animal often falls upon their inner surfaces, and then, of course, unless the rain is very heavy, it is not washed away. It took us something over an hour and a half to reach the edge of the marsh, but once there our task became much easier, for the soft soil showed plentiful evidences of the great brute's passage. Threading our way through the swampy land, we came at last to a ford of the river, and here we could see where the poor wounded animal had lain down in the mud and water in the hope of easing himself of his pain, and could see also how his two faithful companions had assisted him to rise again. We crossed the ford, and took up the spoor on the farther side, and followed it into the marsh-like land beyond. No rain had fallen on this side of the

river, and the blood-marks were consequently
much more frequent.

"All that day we followed the three bulls,
now across open plains, and now through
patches of bush. They seemed to have travelled on almost without stopping, and I no-
ticed that as they went the wounded bull got
up his strength a little. This I could see from
his spoor, which had become firmer, and also
from the fact that the other two had given
up supporting him. At last evening closed
in, and, having travelled some eighteen miles,
we camped, thoroughly tired out.

"Before dawn on the following day we were
up, and the first break of light found us once
more on the spoor. About half - past five
o'clock we reached the place where the elephants had fed and slept. The two unwounded bulls had taken their fill, as the condition
of the neighboring bushes showed, but the
wounded one had eaten nothing. He had spent
the night leaning against a good-sized tree,
which his weight had pushed out of the per-
pendicular. They had not long left this place,
and could not be very far ahead, especially as
the wounded bull was now again so stiff after
his night's rest that for the first few miles the
other two had been obliged to support him.

But elephants go very quick, even when they seem to be travelling slowly, for shrub and creepers that almost stop a man's progress are no hinderance to them. The three had now turned to the left, and were travelling back again in a semicircular line towards the mountains, probably with the idea of working round to their old feeding-grounds on the farther side of the river.

"There was nothing for it but to follow their lead, and accordingly we followed with industry. Through all that long hot day did we tramp, passing quantities of every sort of game, and even coming across the spoor of other elephants. But, in spite of my men's entreaties, I would not turn aside after these. I would have those mighty tusks or none.

"By evening we were quite close to our game, probably within a quarter of a mile, but the bush was dense, and we could see nothing of them, so once more we had to camp, thoroughly disgusted with our luck. That night, just after the moon got up, while I was sitting smoking my pipe with my back against a tree, I heard an elephant trumpet, as though something had startled it, not three hundred yards away. I was very tired, but my curiosity overcame my weariness, so, without say-

ing a word to any of my men, all of whom
were asleep, I took my eight-bore and a few
spare cartridges, and steered towards the sound.
The game path which we had been following
all day ran straight on in the direction from
which the elephant had trumpeted. It was
narrow, but well trodden, and the light struck
down upon it in a straight white line. I crept
along it cautiously for some two hundred yards,
when it suddenly opened into a most beautiful
glade some hundred yards or more in width,
wherein tall grass grew and flat-topped trees
stood singly. With the caution born of long
experience, I watched for a few moments before I entered the glade, and then I saw why
the elephant had trumpeted. There in the
middle of the glade stood a great maned lion.
He stood quite still, making a soft, purring
noise, and waving his tail to and fro. Presently the grass about forty yards on the hither
side of him gave a wide ripple, and a lioness
sprang out of it like a flash, and bounded noise-
lessly up to the lion. Reaching him, the great
cat halted suddenly, and rubbed her head
against his shoulder. Then they both began
to purr loudly, so loudly that I believe that
one might in the stillness have heard them
two hundred yards or more away.

" After a time, while I was still hesitating
what to do, either they got a whiff of my wind,
or they wearied of standing still, and determined to start in search of game. At any rate,
as though moved by a common impulse, they
suddenly bounded away, leap by leap, and vanished in the depths of the forest to the left.
I waited for a little while longer to see if there
were any more yellow-skins about, and, seeing
none, came to the conclusion that the lions
must have frightened the elephants away, and
that I had had my stroll for nothing. But
just as I was turning back I thought I heard
a bough break upon the farther side of the
glade, and, rash as the proceeding was, I followed the sound. I crossed the glade as si-
lently as my own shadow. On its farther side
the path went on. Albeit with many fears, I
went on too. The jungle growth was so thick
here that it almost met overhead, leaving so
small a passage for the light that I could
scarcely see to grope my way along. Presently, however, it widened, and then opened
into a second glade slightly smaller than the
first, and there, on the farther side of it, about
eighty yards from me, stood the three enormous elephants.

" They stood thus : Immediately opposite and

facing me was the wounded one-tusked bull.
He was leaning his bulk against a dead thorn-
tree, the only one in the place, and looked very
sick indeed. Near him stood the second bull,
as though keeping a watch over him. The
third elephant was a good deal nearer to me,
and broadside on. While I was still staring
at them this elephant suddenly walked off and
vanished down a path in the bush to the right.

"There were now two things to be done:
either I could go back to the camp, and advance upon the elephants at dawn, or I could
attack them at once. The first was, of course,
by far the wisest and safest course. To go for
one elephant by moonlight, and single-handed,
is a sufficiently rash proceeding; to tackle three
was little short of lunacy. But, on the other
hand, I knew that they would be on the march
again before daylight, and there might come
another day of weary trudging before I could
catch them up, or they might escape me altogether.

"'No,' I thought to myself, 'faint heart
never won fair tusk. I'll risk it, and have a
slap at them. But how?' I could not advance across the open, for they would see me,
clearly the only thing to do was to creep
round in the shadow of the bush, and try to

come upon them. So I started. Seven or eight minutes of careful stalking brought me to the mouth of the path down which the third elephant had walked. The other two were now about fifty yards from me, and the nature of the wall of bush was such that I could not see how to get nearer to them without being discovered. I hesitated, and peeped down the path which the elephant had followed. About five yards in it took a turn round a bush. I thought that I would just have a look behind it, and advanced, expecting that I should be able to catch a sight of the elephant's tail.

"As it happened, however, I met his trunk coming round the corner. It is very disconcerting to see an elephant's trunk when you expect to see his tail, and for a moment I stood paralyzed almost under the vast brute's head, for he was not five yards from me. He, too, halted, having either seen or winded me, probably the latter, and then threw up his trunk and trumpeted preparatory to a charge. I was in for it now, for I could not escape either to the right or left on account of the bush, and I did not dare turn my back. So I did the only thing that I could do, raised the rifle and fired at the black mass of his chest. It was too dark for me to pick a shot ; I could only brown it, as it were.

"The shot rung out like thunder on the quiet air, and the elephant answered it with a scream, and then dropped his trunk, and stood for a second or two as still as though he had been cut in stone. I confess that I lost my head— I ought to have fired my second barrel, but I did not. Instead of doing so, I rapidly opened my rifle, pulled out the old cartridge from the right barrel and replaced it. But before I could snap the breech to, the bull was at me. I saw his great trunk fly up like a brown beam, and I waited no longer. Turning, I fled for dear life, and after me thundered the elephant. Right into the open glade I ran, and then, thank Heaven, just as he was coming up with me, the bullet took effect on him. He had been shot right through the heart, or lungs, and down he fell with a crash, stone-dead.

" But in escaping from Scylla I had run into the jaws of Charybdis. I heard the elephant fall, and glanced round. Straight in front of me, and not fifteen paces away, were the other two bulls. They were staring about, and at that moment they caught sight of me. Then they came, the pair of them—came like thunderbolts, and from different angles. I had

only time to snap my rifle to, lift it, and fire,
almost at haphazard, at the head of the nearest, the unwounded bull.

" Now as you know, in the case of the African elephant, whose scull is convex, and not
concave like that of the Indian, this is always
a most risky, and very frequently a perfectly
useless shot. The bullet loses itself in the
masses of bone, that is all. But there is one
little vital place, and should the bullet happen
to strike there, it will follow the channel of the
nostrils—at least I suppose it is the nostrils—
and reach the brain. And it was what happened in this case ; the ball struck the fatal
spot in the region of the eye and travelled to
the brain. Down came the great bull all of
a heap, and rolled on to his side as dead as a
stone. I swung round at that instant to face
the third, the monster bull with one tusk that
I had wounded two days before. He was already almost over me, and in the dim moonlight seemed to tower above me like a house.
I lifted the rifle and pulled at his neck. It
would not go off. Then, in a flash as it were,
I remembered that it was on the half-cock.
The lock of the barrel was a little weak, and
a few days before, in firing at a cow eland,
the left barrel had jarred off at the shock of

the discharge of the right, knocking me backward with the recoil; so after that I had kept it on the half-cock till I actually wanted to fire it.

"I gave one desperate bound to the right, and, my lame leg notwithstanding, I believe that few men could have made a better jump. At any rate it was none too soon, for as I jumped I felt the wind made by the tremendous downward stroke of the monster's trunk. Then I ran for it.

"I ran like the wind, still keeping hold of my gun, however. My idea, so far as I could be said to have any fixed idea, was to bolt down the pathway up which I had come, like a rabbit down a burrow, trusting that he would lose sight of me in the uncertain light. I sped across the glade. Fortunately the bull, being wounded, could not go full speed; but wounded or no, he could go quite as fast as I could. I was unable to gain an inch, and away we went with just about three feet between our separate extremities. We were at the other side now, and a glance served to show me that I had miscalculated and overshot the opening. To reach it now was hopeless; I should have blundered straight into the elephant. So I did the only thing I could do: I swerved like a coursed hare, and started off round the edge of the glade, seeking for some opening into which I could plunge. This gave me a moment's start, for the bull could not turn as quickly as I could, and I made the most of it. But no opening could I see; the bush was like a wall. We were speeding round the edge of the glade, and the elephant was coming up again. Now he was within about six feet, and now as he trumpeted, or rather screamed, I could feel the fierce hot blast of his breath strike upon my head. Heavens! how it frightened me! We were three parts round the glade now, and about fifty yards ahead was the single large dead thorn-tree against which the bull had been leaning. I spurted for it; it was my last chance of safety. But spurt as I would, it seemed hours before I got there. Putting out my right hand, I swung round the tree, thus bringing myself face to face with the elephant. I had not time to lift the rifle to fire, I had barely time to cock it and run sideways and backward, when he was on to me. Crash! he came, striking the tree full with his forehead. It snapped like a carrot about forty inches from the ground. Fortunately I was clear of the trunk, but one of the dead branches struck me on the chest and swept me to the ground. I fell upon my back, and the elephant blundered past me as I lay. More by instinct than anything else I lifted my rifle with one hand and pulled the trigger. It exploded, and, as I afterwards discovered, the bullet struck him in the ribs. But the recoil of the heavy rifle held thus was very severe; it bent my arm up and sent the butt with a thud against the top of my shoulder and the side of my neck, for the moment quite paralyzing me, and causing the weapon to jump from my grasp. Meanwhile the bull was rushing on. He travelled for some twenty paces, and then suddenly he stopped. Faintly I reflected that he was coming back to finish me, but even the prospect of imminent and dreadful death could not rouse me into action. I was utterly spent; I could not move.

"Idly, almost indifferently, I watched his movements. For a moment he stood still, then he trumpeted till the welkin rang, and then very slowly, and with great dignity, he knelt down. At this point I swooned away.

"When I came to myself again I saw from the moon that I must have been insensible for quite two hours. I was drenched with dew and shivering all over. At first I could not think where I was, when, on lifting my head, I saw the outline of the one-tusked bull still

kneeling some five-and-twenty paces from me.
Then I remembered. Slowly I raised myself,
and was instantly taken with a violent sick-
ness, the result of over-exertion, after which I
nearly fainted a second time. Presently I grew
better, and considered the position. Two of
the elephants were, as I knew, dead; but how
about No. 3? There he knelt in majesty in
the lonely moonlight. The question was, was
he resting, or dead? I got on my hands and
knees, loaded my rifle, and painfully crept a
few paces nearer. I could see his eye now,
for the moonlight fell full upon it; it was
open, and rather prominent. I crouched and
watched; the eyelid did not move, nor did the
great brown body, or the trunk, or the ear, or
the tail—nothing moved. Then I knew that
he must be dead.

"I crept up to him—still keeping the rifle
well forward—and gave him a thump, reflecting as I did so how very near I had been to
being 'thumpee instead of thumper.' He never
stirred; he certainly was dead, though to this
day I do not know if it was my random shot
that killed him, or if he died from concussion
of the brain consequent upon the tremendous
shock of his contact with the tree. Anyhow,
there he was. Cold and beautiful he lay, or

rather knelt, as the poet neatly puts it. Indeed, I do not think that I have ever seen a
sight more imposing in its way than that
mighty beast crouched in majestic death and
shone upon by the lonely moon. While I
stood admiring the whole scene, and heartily
congratulating myself upon my escape, I once
more began to feel sick. Accordingly, without waiting to examine the other two bulls, I
staggered off back to the camp, which in due
course I reached in safety. Everybody in it
was asleep. I did not wake them, but, having swallowed a mouthful of brandy, I threw
off my coat and shoes, rolled myself up in a
blanket, and was soon fast asleep. When I
woke it was already light, and at first I
thought that, like Joseph, I had dreamed a
dream. At that moment, however, I turned
my head, and quickly knew that it was no
dream, for my neck and face were so stiff
from the blow of the butt end of the rifle
that it was agony to move them. I collapsed
for a minute or two. Gobo and another man,
wrapped up like a couple of monks in their
blankets, thinking that I was still asleep, were
crouched over a little fire they had made—for
the morning was damp and chilly—and holding sweet converse.

"Gobo said that he was getting tired of running. after elephants which they never caught. Macumazahn (that is myself) was without doubt a man of parts and of some skill in shooting, but also he was a fool. None but a fool would run so fast and far after elephants which it was impossible to catch when they kept cutting the spoor of fresh ones. He certainly was a fool; but he must not be allowed to continue in his folly, and he, Gobo, had determined to put a stop to it. He should refuse to accompany him any farther on so mad a hunt.

"Yes, the other answered, the poor man certainly was sick in his head, and it was quite time that they checked his folly while they still had a patch of skin left upon their feet. Moreover, he, for his part, certainly did not like this country of Wambe's, which really was full of ghosts. Only the last night he had heard the spooks at work; they were out shooting; at least it sounded as though they were. It was very queer, but perhaps their lunatic of a master—

"'Gobo, you scoundrel!' I shouted out at this juncture, sitting bolt-upright on the blankets, 'stop idling there, and make me some coffee.'

"Up sprang Gobo and his friend, and in half

a moment were respectfully skipping about in
a manner that contrasted well with the lordly
contempt of their previous conversation.   But
all the same they were in earnest in what they
said about hunting the elephants any farther,
for before I had finished my coffee they came
to me in a body, and said that if I wanted to
follow those elephants I must follow them by
myself, for they would not go.

"I argued with them, and affected to be
much put out.   The elephants were close at
hand, I said; I was sure of it; I had heard
them trumpet in the night.

"Yes, answered the men, mysteriously; they
too had heard things in the night—things not
nice to hear; they had heard the spooks out
shooting, and would no longer remain in a
country so vilely haunted.

"'It was nonsense,' I replied. 'If ghosts
went out shooting, surely they would use air-
guns and not black powder, and one would not
hear an air-gun.   Well, if they were cowards,
and would not come, of course I could not
force them to, but I would make a bargain
with them.   They should follow those elephants for one half hour more, then if we
failed to come upon them I would abandon
the pursuit, and we would go straight to

Wambe, chief of the Matuku, and give him hongo.'

"To this compromise the men readily agreed. Accordingly about half an hour later we struck our camp and started, and notwithstanding my aches and bruises I do not think that I ever felt in better spirits in my life. It is something to wake up in the morning and remember that in the dead of night one has, single-handed, given battle to and overthrown three of the largest elephants in Africa, slaying them with three bullets. Such a feat had never to my knowledge been done before, and on that particular morning I felt a very 'tall man of my hands' indeed. The only thing that I feared was that should I ever come to tell the story, nobody would believe it, for when a strange story is told by a hunter, people are apt to think it is necessarily a lie, instead of being only probably so.*

---

* For the satisfaction of any who may be so disbelieving as to take this view of Mr. Quatermain's story, the Editor may state that a gentleman with whom he is acquainted, and whose veracity he believes to be beyond doubt, not long ago described to him how he chanced to kill *four* African elephants with four consecutive bullets. Two of these elephants were charging him simultaneously, and out of the four, three were killed with the head-shot, a very uncommon thing in the case of the African elephant.—EDITOR.

"Well, we passed on, till, having crossed the first glade where I had seen the lions, we reached the neck of bush that separated it from the second glade where the dead elephants were. And here I began to take elaborate precautions, among others ordering Gobo to keep some yards ahead and look out sharp, as I thought that the elephants might be about. He obeyed my instructions with a superior smile, and pushed ahead. Presently I saw him pull up as though he had been shot, and begin to faintly snap his fingers.

"'What is it?' I whispered.

"'The elephant, the great elephant with one tusk, kneeling down.'

"I crept up beside him. There knelt the bull as I had left him last night, and there, too, lay the other bulls.

"'Do these elephants sleep?' I whispered to the astonished Gobo.

"'Yes, Macumazahn, they sleep.'

"'Nay, Gobo, they are dead.'

"'Dead? How can they be dead? Who killed them?'

"'What do people call me, Gobo?'

"'They call you Macumazahn.'

"'And what does Macumazahn mean?'

"'It means the man who keeps his eyes open, the man who gets up in the night.'

"'Yes, and I am that man. Look, you idle, lazy cowards. While you slept last night I rose, and alone I hunted those great elephants, and slew them by the moonlight. To each of them I gave one bullet and only one, and it fell dead. Look,' and I advanced into the glade, 'here is my spoor, and here is the spoor of the great bull charging after me, and there is the tree that I took refuge behind. See, the elephant shattered it in his charge. Oh, you cowards, you who would give up the chase while the blood-spoor steamed beneath your nostrils! See what I did single-handed while you slept, and be ashamed!'

"'Ou,' said the man—'ou. Koos, koos, y umcool!' (Chief, mighty chief!); and then they held their tongues, and, going up to the three dead beasts, gazed upon them in silence.

"But after that those men looked upon me with awe as being almost more than mortal. No mere man, they said, could have slain those three elephants alone in the night-time. 'I never had any further trouble with them. I believe that if I had told them to jump over a precipice and that they would take no harm, they would have believed me.

"Well, I went up and examined the bulls. Such tusks as they had I never saw, and never

shall see again. It took us all day to cut them
out, and when they reached Delagoa Bay, as
they did ultimately, though not in my keeping,
the single tusk of the big bull scaled one hundred and sixty pounds, and the four other tusks
averaged ninety-nine and a half pounds — a
most wonderful, indeed an almost unprecedent-
ed, lot of ivory.* Unfortunately I was forced
to saw the big tusk in two, otherwise we could
not have carried it."

"Oh, Quatermain, you barbarian!" I broke
in here, "the idea of spoiling such a tusk!
Why, I would have kept it whole if I had
been obliged to drag it myself."

"Oh, yes, young man," he answered, "it is
all very well for you to talk like that, but if
you had found yourself in the position which
it was my privilege to occupy a few hours afterwards, it is my belief that you would have
thrown the tusks away altogether and taken
to your heels."

"Oh," said Good, "so that isn't the end of
the yarn? A very good yarn, Quatermain, by
the way — I couldn't have made up a better
one myself."

The old gentleman looked at Good severe-

---

* The largest elephant tusk of which the Editor has any certain knowledge scaled one hundred and fifty pounds.—EDITOR.

ly, for it irritated him to be chaffed about his stories.

"I don't know what you mean, Good. I don't see that there is any comparison between a true story of adventure and the preposterous tales which you invent about ibex hanging by their horns. No, it is not the end of the story; the most exciting part is to come. But I have talked enough for to-night; and if you go on in that way, Good, it will be some time before I begin again."

"Sorry I spoke, I'm sure," said Good, humbly, "Let's have a split to show that there is no ill-feeling." And they did.

CHAPTER V.

THE MESSAGE OF MAIWA.

On the following evening we once more dined together, and Quatermain, after some pressure, for Good's remark still rankled in his breast, was persuaded to continue his story.

"At last," he went on, "a few minutes before sunset, the task was finished. We had labored at it all day, stopping only once for dinner; for it is no easy matter to hew out five such tusks as those which now lay before me in a white and gleaming line. It was a dinner worth eating, too, I can tell you, for we dined off the heart of the great one-tusked bull, which was so big that the man whom I sent inside the elephant to look for his heart had to remove it in two pieces. We cut it into slices and fried it with fat, and I never tasted heart to equal it, for the meat seemed to melt in one's mouth. By the way, I examined the jaw of the elephant; it had never had but one tusk; the other had not been broken off, nor was it present in a rudimentary form.

"Well, there lay the five beauties, or, rather, four of them, for Gobo and another man were engaged in sawing the grand one in two. I had at last, with many sighs, ordered them to do this, but not until I had by practical experiment proved that it was impossible to carry it in any other way. One hundred and sixty pounds of solid ivory, or rather more in its green state, is too great a weight for two men to carry for long across a broken country. I sat watching the job and smoking the pipe of contentment, when suddenly the bush opened, and a very handsome and dignified native girl, apparently about twenty years of age, stood before me, carrying a basket of green mealies upon her head.

"Although I was rather surprised to see a native girl in such a wild spot, and, so far as I knew, a long way from any kraal, the matter did not attract my particular notice; I merely called to one of the men and told him to bargain with the woman for the mealies, and ask her if there were any more to be had in the neighborhood. Then I turned my head and continued to superintend the cutting of the tusk. Presently a shadow fell upon me.

I looked up and saw that the girl was standing before me, the basket of mealies still on her head.

"'Marême, Marême,' she said, gently clapping her hands together. The word 'Marême' among these Matuku (though she was no Matuku) answers to the Zulu 'Koos,' and the clapping of hands is a form of salutation very common among the tribes of the Basutu race.

"'What is it, girl?' I asked her in Sisutu. 'Are those mealies for sale?'

"'No, great white hunter,' she answered in Zulu; 'I bring them as a gift.'

"'Good!' I replied. 'Put them down.'

"'A gift for a gift, white man.'

"'Ah!' I grumbled, 'the old story—nothing for nothing in this wicked world. What do you want—beads?'

"She nodded, and I was about to tell one of the men to go and fetch some from one of the packs, when she checked me.

"'A gift from the giver's own hand is twice a gift,' she said; and I thought that she spoke meaningly.

"'You mean that you want me to give them to you myself?'

"'Surely.'

"I rose to go with her. 'How is it that,

being of the Matuku, you speak in the Zulu
tongue?' I asked, suspiciously.

" 'I am not of the Matuku,' she answered,
as soon as we were out of hearing of the men.
'I am of the people of Nala, whose tribe is the
Butiana tribe, and who lives there,' and she
pointed over the mountain. 'Also, I am one
of the wives of Wambe,' and her eyes flashed
as she said the name.

" 'And how did you come here?'

" 'On my feet,' she answered, laconically.

" We reached the packs, and, undoing one of
them, I extracted a handful of beads. 'Now,'
said I, 'a gift for a gift. Hand over the mealies.'

" She took the beads without even looking
at them, which struck me as curious, and, putting the basket of mealies on the ground, emptied it.

" At the bottom of the basket were some cu-
riously shaped green leaves, something like the
leaves of the gutta-percha tree in shape, only
somewhat thicker, and of a more fleshy sub-
stance. As though by hazard, the girl picked
one of these leaves out of the basket and smelt
at it; then she handed it to me. I took the
leaf, and, supposing that she wished me to
smell it also, was about to oblige her by doing

so, when my eye fell upon some curious red
scratches on the green surface of the leaf.

"'Ah!' said the girl (whose name, by the
way, was Maiwa), speaking beneath her breath;
'read the signs, white man.'

"Without answering her I continued to stare
at the leaf. It had been scratched, or rather
written upon, with something sharp, such as a
nail, and wherever this instrument had touched
it the acid juice oozing through the outer skin
had turned a rusty blood-color. Presently I
found the beginning of the scrawl, and read
this, written in English, and covering the surface of the leaf and of two others that were in
the basket:

"'I hear that a white man is hunting in the Matuku
country. This is to warn him to fly over the mountain to
Nala. Wambe sends an Impi at daybreak to eat him up
because he has hunted before bringing hongo. For God's
sake, whoever you are, try to help me! I have been the
slave of this devil Wambe for nearly seven years, and am
beaten and tortured continually. He murdered all the rest
of us, but kept me because I could work iron. Maiwa, his
wife, takes this; she is flying to Nala, her father, because
Wambe killed her child. Try and get Nala to attack
Wambe. Maiwa can guide them over the mountain. You
won't come for nothing, for the stockade of Wambe's private kraal is made of elephants' tusks. For God's sake
don't desert me, or I shall kill myself! I can bear this no
longer.   JOHN EVERY.'

" 'Great heavens!' I gasped. 'Every—why, it must be my old friend.' The girl, or rather the woman, Maiwa pointed to the other side of the leaf where there was some more writing. It ran thus: 'I have just heard that the white man is called Macumazahn. If so, it must be my old friend Quatermain. Pray God it is, for I know he won't desert an old chum in such a fix as I am. It isn't that I'm afraid of dying; I don't care if I die; but I want to get a chance at Wambe first.'

" 'No, old boy,' thought I to myself, 'it isn't likely that I am going to leave you there while there is a chance of getting you out. I have played fox before now—there's still a double or two left in me. I must make a plan, that's all. And then there's that stockade of tusks. I am not going to leave that either.' Then I spoke to the woman.

" 'You are called Maiwa.'

" 'It is so.'

" 'You are the daughter of Nala and the wife of Wambe.'

" 'It is so.'

" 'You fly from Wambe to Nala.'

" 'I do.'

" 'Why do you fly? Stay, I would give an order,' and, calling to Gobo, I ordered him to get the men ready for instant departure. The woman, who, as I have said, was quite young and very handsome, put her hand into a kind of little pouch made of antelope hide which she wore fastened round the waist, and to my horror drew from it the withered hand of a child which had evidently been carefully dried in the smoke.

" ' I fly for this cause,' she answered, holding the poor little hand towards me. ' See now, I bore a child. Wambe was its father, and for eighteen months the child lived, and I loved it. But Wambe loves not his children; he kills them all; he fears lest they should grow up to slay one so wicked; and he would have killed this child also, but I begged its life. One day some soldiers passing the hut saw the child and saluted him, calling him the " chief who soon shall be." Wambe heard and was mad. He smote the babe, and it wept. Then he said that it should weep for good cause. Among the things that he had stolen from the white men whom he slew is a trap that will hold lions. So strong is the trap that four men must stand on it, two on either side, before it can be opened.' "

Here old Quatermain broke off suddenly.

"Look here, you fellows," he said, "I can't
bear to go on with this part of the story, because I never could stand either seeing or talking of the sufferings of children. You can
guess what that devil did and what the poor
mother was forced to witness. Would you believe it, she told me the tale without a tremor,
in the most matter-of-fact way. Only I no-
ticed that her eyelid quivered all the time.

"'Well,' I said, as unconcernedly as though
I had been talking of the death of a lamb,
though inwardly I was sick with horror and
boiling with rage, 'and what do you mean to
do about the matter, Maiwa, wife of Wambe?'

"'I mean to do this, white man,' she answered, drawing herself up to her full height
and speaking in tones as hard as steel and as
cool as ice. 'I mean to work and work and
work, to bring this to pass, and to bring that
to pass, until at length it comes to pass that
with these living eyes I behold Wambe dying
the death that he gave to his child and my
child.'

"'Well said,' I answered.

"'Ay, well said, Macumazahn; well said,
and not easily forgotten. Who could forget?
See where this dead hand rests against my

side; so once it rested when alive. And now,
though it is dead, now every night it creeps
from its nest, and strokes my hair, and clasps
my fingers in its tiny palm. Every night it
does this, fearing lest I should forget. Oh,
my child! my child! ten days ago I held thee
to my breast, and now this alone remains of
thee!' and she kissed the dead hand and shiv-
ered, but never a tear did she weep. 'See
now,' she went on, 'the white man, the prisoner at Wambe's kraal, he was kind to me.
He loved the child that is dead; yes, he wept
when its father slew it, and at the risk of his
own life told Wambe, my husband—ah yes,
my husband!—that which he is! He, too, it
was who made a plan. He said to me, " Go,
Maiwa, after the custom of thy people, go purify thyself in the bush alone, having touched
a dead one. Say to Wambe thou goest to purify thyself alone for fifteen days, according
to the custom of the people. Then fly to thy
father Nala, and stir him up to war against
Wambe for the sake of the child that is dead."
This then he said, and his words seemed good
to me, and that same night ere I left to purify
myself came news that a white man hunted
in the country, and Wambe, being mad with
drink, grew very wrath, and gave orders that

an Impi should be gathered to slay the white man and his people, and seize his goods. Then did the "Smiter of Iron" [Every] write the message on the green leaves, and bid me seek thee out and show forth the matter, that thou mightest save thyself by flight; and behold, this thing have I done, Macumazahn, the hunter, the Slayer of Elephants.'

" ' Ah,' I said, ' I thank thee. And how many men be there in the Impi of Wambe?'

" ' A hundred of men and half a hundred.'

" ' And where is the Impi?'

" ' There to the north. It follows on thy spoor. I saw it pass yesterday, but myself I guessed that thou wouldst be nigher to the mountain and came this way and found thee. To-morrow at the daybreak will the slayers be here.'

" ' Very possibly,' I thought to myself; ' but they won't find Macumazahn. I have half a mind to put some strychnine into the carcasses of those elephants for their especial benefit, though.' I knew that they would stop to eat the elephants, as indeed they did, to our great gain, but I abandoned the idea of poisoning them, because I was rather short of strychnine."

" Or because you did not like to play the trick, Quatermain," I suggested, with a laugh.

" I said because I had not enough strychnine. It would take a great deal of strychnine to effectually poison three elephants," answered the old gentleman, testily.

I said nothing further, but I smiled, knowing that old Allan could never have resorted to such an artifice, however severe his strait. But that was his way; he always made himself out to be a most unmerciful person.

" Well," he went on, " at that moment Gobo came up and announced that we were ready to march. ' I am glad that you are ready,' I said; ' because if you don't march, and march quick, you will never march again, that is all. Wambe has an Impi out to kill us, and it will be here presently.'

" Gobo turned positively green, and his knees knocked together. ' Ah, what did I say?' he exclaimed. ' Fate walks about loose in Wambe's country.'

" ' Very good; now all you have got to do is to walk a little quicker than he does. No, no; you don't leave those elephant tusks behind. I am not going to part with them, I can tell you.'

" Gobo said no more, but hastily directed the men to take up their loads, and then asked which way we were to run.

" ' Ah,' I said to Maiwa, ' which way ?'

" ' There,' she answered, pointing towards the great mountain spur which towered up into the sky some forty miles away, separating the territories of Nala and Wambe. ' There, below that small peak, is one place where men may pass, and one only. Also, it can easily be blocked from above. If men pass not there, then they must go round the great peak of the mountain two days' journey and half a day.'

" ' And how far is the peak from us ?'

" ' All to-night shall you walk and all to-morrow, and if you walk fast, at sunset shall you stand on the peak.'

" I whistled, for that meant a five-and-forty miles' trudge without sleep. Then I called to the men to take each of them as much cooked elephant's meat as he could conveniently carry. I did the same myself, and forced the woman Maiwa to eat some as we went. This I did with difficulty, for at that time she seemed neither to sleep, nor eat, nor rest, so fiercely was she set on vengeance.

" Then we started, Maiwa guiding us. After going for some half-hour over gradually rising

ground we found ourselves on the farther edge
of a great bush-clad depression, something like
the bottom of a lake. This depression through
which we had been travelling was to a very
great extent covered with bush; indeed, almost
altogether so, except where it was pitted with
glades such as that wherein I had shot the
elephants.

"At the top of this slope Maiwa halted, and,
putting her hand over her eyes, looked back.
Presently she touched me on the arm, and
pointed over the sea of forest towards a comparatively vacant space of country some six
or seven miles away. I looked, and suddenly
I saw something flash in the red rays of the
setting sun. A pause, and then another quick
flash.

"'What is it?' I asked.

"'It is the spears of Wambe's Impi, and they
travel fast,' she answered, coolly.

"I suppose my face showed how little I
liked the news, for she went on:

"'Fear not; they will stay to feast upon
the elephants, and while they feast we shall
journey. We may yet escape.'

"After that we turned and pushed on again,
till at length it grew so dark that we had to
wait for the rising of the moon, which lost us

time, though it gave us rest. Fortunately, none of the men had seen that ominous flashing of the spears; if they had, I doubt if I could have kept control of them. As it was, they travelled faster than I had ever known loaded natives go before, so thorough-paced was their desire to see the last of Wambe's country. I, however, took the precaution to march last of all, fearing lest they should throw away their loads to lighten themselves, or, worse still, the tusks; for these kind of fellows would be capable of throwing anything away if their own skins were at stake. If the pious Æneas, whose story you were reading to me the other night, had been a mongrel Delagoa Bay native, Anchises would have had a poor chance of getting out of Troy, that is, if he was already known to have made a satisfactory will.

"At the moonrise we started on again, and with short occasional halts travelled till dawn, when we were forced to rest and eat. Starting once more, about half-past five, we crossed the river at noon. Then began the long toilsome ascent through thick bush, the same in which I shot the bull buffalo, only some twenty miles to the west of the spot, and not more than twenty-five miles on the hither side of

Wambe's kraal. There were six or seven miles
of this dense bush, and hard work it was to
get through it. Next came a belt of scattered
forest, which was easier to pass, though in revenge the ground was steeper. This was about
two miles wide, and we passed it by about
four in the afternoon. Above this scattered
bush lay a long steep slope of boulder-strewn
ground, which ran up to the foot of the little
peak some three miles away. As footsore and
weary we emerged on to this inhospitable plain,
some of the men, looking round, caught sight
of the spears of Wambe's Impi coming rapidly
along not more than a mile behind us.

" At first there was a panic, and the bearers
tried to throw off their loads and run, but I
harangued them, calling out to them that I
would certainly shoot the first man who did
so, and that if they would but trust in me I
would bring them through the mess. Now
ever since I had killed those three elephants
single-handed I had gained great influence
over these men, and they listened to me. So
off we went as hard as ever we could go; the
members of the Alpine Club would not have
been in it with us. We made the boulders
burn, as a Frenchman would say. When we
had done about a mile, the spears began to

emerge from the belt of scattered bush, and the whoop of their bearers as they viewed us broke upon our ears. Quick as our pace had been before, it grew much quicker now, for terror lent wings to my gallant crew. But they were sorely tired, and the loads were heavy, so that run, or rather climb, as we would, Wambe's soldiers, a scrubby-looking lot of men with big spears, small shields, but without plumes, climbed considerably faster. The last mile of that pleasing chase was like a fox hunt, we being the fox, and always in view. What astonished me was the extraordinary endurance and activity shown by Maiwa. She never even flagged. I think that girl's muscles must have been made of iron, or perhaps it was the strength of her will that supported her. At any rate, she reached the foot of the peak second, poor Gobo, who was an excellent hand at running away, being first.

" Presently I came panting up, and glanced at the ascent. Before us was a wall of rock about one· hundred and fifty feet in height, upon which the strata were so laid as to form a series of projections sufficiently resembling steps to make the ascent, comparatively speaking, easy, except at one spot where it was necessary to climb over a projecting angle of cliff

and bear a little to the left. It was not a
really difficult place, but what made it awkward was that immediately beneath this projection was a deep fissure or donga, on the
brink of which we now stood, originally dug
out, no doubt, by the rush of water from the
peak and cliff. This gulf beneath would, at
the critical point, be trying to the nerves of a
weak-headed climber, and so it proved in the
result. After the projecting angle was passed,
the remainder of the ascent was very simple.
At the summit, however, the brow of the cliff
hung over, and was pierced by a single narrow
path cut through it by water in such fashion
that a single boulder rolled into it at the top
would make the cliff quite impassable to people
without ropes.

"Wambe's soldiers were at this moment
about a thousand yards from us, so it was evi-
dent that we had no time to lose. I at once
ordered the men to commence the ascent, the
girl Maiwa, who was familiar with the pass,
going first to show them the way. Accordingly they began to mount with alacrity, pushing and lifting their loads in front of them.
When the first of them, led by Maiwa, reached
the projecting angle, they put down their loads
upon a ledge of rock and clambered over. Once

up, by going on their stomachs on a boulder,
they could reach the loads which were held
up to them by the men beneath, and in this
way drag them up over the awkward place,
whence they were easily carried to the top.
But all of this took time, and meanwhile the
soldiers were coming up fast, screaming and
brandishing their big spears. They were now
within about four hundred yards, and several
loads, together with all the tusks, had yet to
be got over the rock. I was still standing at
the bottom of the cliff, shouting out directions
to the men above, but it occurred to me that
it would soon be time to move. Before doing
so, however, I thought that it might be well
to try and produce a moral effect upon the
advancing enemy. In my hand I held a Winchester repeating carbine, but the distance was
too great for me to use it with effect, so I
turned to Gobo, who was shivering with terror at my side, and, handing him the carbine,
took from him my express. The enemy was
now about three hundred and fifty yards away,
and the express was only sighted to three hundred. Still I knew that it could be trusted
for the extra fifty yards. Running in front
of Wambe's soldiers were two men—captains,
I suppose—one of them very tall. I put up

the three-hundred-yard flap, and, sitting down
with my back against the rock, I drew a long
breath to steady myself, and covered the tall
man, giving him a full sight. Feeling that I
was on him, I pulled, and before the sound of
the striking bullet could reach my ears, I saw
the man throw up his arms and pitch forward
on to his head. His companion stopped dead,
giving me a fair chance. I rapidly covered
him, and fired the left barrel. He turned
round once, and then sank down in a heap.

"This caused the enemy to hesitate; they
had never seen men killed at such a distance
before, and thought that there was something
uncanny about the performance. Taking advantage of the lull, I gave the express back to
Gobo, and, slinging the Winchester repeater
over my back, I began to climb the cliff. When
we reached the projecting angle all the loads
were over, but the tusks still had to be passed
up, and this, owing to their weight and the
smoothness of their surface, was a very difficult task. Of course I ought to have abandoned the tusks; often and often have I since
reproached myself for not doing so. Indeed,
I think that my obstinacy about them was
downright sinful, but I always was obstinate
about things, and I could not bear the idea of

leaving those splendid tusks which had cost
me so much pains and danger to come by.
Well, it nearly cost me my life also, and did
cost poor Gobo his, as will shortly be seen, to
say nothing of the loss inflicted by my rifle
on the enemy. When I reached the projection I found that the men were trying, with
their usual stupidity, to hand up the tusks
point first. Now the result of this was that
those above had nothing to grip except the
round polished surface of the ivory, and this,
in the position in which they were, did not
give sufficient hold to enable them to lift the
weight. I told them to reverse the tusks and
push them up, so that the rough and hollow
ends came to the hands of the men above. This
they did, and the first two were got up in
safety.

" At this point, looking behind me, I saw the
Matukus streaming up the slope in a rough,
extended order, and not more than a hundred yards away. Cocking the Winchester, I
opened fire on them. I don't quite know how
many I missed, but I do know that I never shot
better in my life. It was exactly like pheasant-
shooting at a hot corner. I had to keep shift-
ing myself from one to the other, firing almost
without getting a sight—that is, by the eye

alone, after the fashion of the experts who break
glass balls. But quick as the work was, men
fell thick, and by the time that I had emptied
the carbine of its twelve cartridges the advance was for the moment checked. I rapidly pushed in some more cartridges, and hardly
had I done so when the enemy, seeing that we
were about to escape them altogether, came
on once more with a tremendous yell. By this
time the two halves of the single tusk of the
great bull alone remained to be passed up. I
fired, and fired as effectively as before, but notwithstanding all that I could do, some men escaped my hail of bullets, and began to ascend
the cliff. Presently my rifle was again empty.
I slung it over my back, and, drawing my revolver, turned to make a bolt of it, the attack-
ers being now quite close; as I did so a spear
struck the cliff close to my head. The last
half of the tusk was now vanishing over the
rock, and I sung out to Gobo and the other
man who had been pushing it up to vanish
after it. Gobo, poor fellow, required no second invitation; indeed, his haste was his undoing. He went at the projecting rock with
a bound. The end of the tusk was still projecting over, and instead of grasping the rock,
he caught at it. It twisted in his hand; he

slipped, he fell. With one wild shriek he vanished into the abyss beneath, his falling body brushing me as it passed.

"For a moment we stood aghast, and presently the dull thud of his fall smote heavily on our ears. Poor fellow, he had met the Fate which, as he had declared, walked about loose in Wambe's country. Then, with an oath, the remaining man sprang at the rock, and clambered over it in safety. Aghast at the awfulness of what had happened, I stood still, till I saw the great blade of a Matuku spear pass up between my feet. That brought me to my senses, and I began to clamber up the rock like a cat. I was half-way round it. Already I had clasped the hand of that brave girl Maiwa, who had come down to help me, the men having scrambled forward with the ivory, when I felt a hand seize my ankle.

"'Pull, Maiwa, pull!' I gasped; and she certainly did pull. Maiwa was a very muscular woman, and never before did I so keenly appreciate the advantages of the physical development of females. She tugged at my left arm, the savage below tugged at my right leg, till I began to realize that something must ere long give way. Luckily I retained my presence of mind, like the man who, when a fire

broke out in his house, threw his mother-in-law
out of the window and carried the mattress
down-stairs. My right hand was still free, and
in it was my revolver, which was secured to
my wrist by a leather thong. It was cocked,
and I simply held it downward and fired. The
result was instantaneous—and so far as I was
concerned, most satisfactory. The bullet hit
the man beneath me somewhere, I am sure I
don't know where. At any rate, he let go of
my leg, and plunged headlong into the gulf
beneath to join Gobo. In another moment I
was on the top of the rock, and going up the
remaining steps like a lamp-lighter. A single
other soldier appeared in pursuit, but one of my
boys at the top fired my elephant gun at him.
I don't know if he hit him or only frightened
him; at any rate, he vanished whence he came.
I do know, however, that he very nearly hit
me, for I felt the wind of the bullet. Another
thirty seconds, and I and the woman Maiwa
were at the top of the cliff, panting but safe.

"My men, being directed thereto by Maiwa,
had most fortunately rolled up some big boulders which lay about, and with these we soon
managed to block the passage through the
overhanging ridge of rock in such fashion that
the soldiers below could not possibly climb

over it. Indeed, so far as I could see, they did not even try to do so; the heart was out of them, as the Zulus say.

"Then, having rested for a few moments, we took up the loads, including the tusks of ivory that had cost us so dear, and in silence marched on for a couple of miles or more, till we reached a patch of dense bush. And here, being utterly exhausted, we camped for the night, taking the precaution, however, of setting a guard to watch against any attempt at surprise.

CHAPTER VI.

THE PLAN OF CAMPAIGN.

"Notwithstanding all that we had gone through, perhaps, indeed, on account of it—for I was thoroughly worn out—I slept that night as soundly as poor Gobo, round whose crushed body the hyenas would now be prowling. Rising refreshed at dawn we went on our way towards Nala's kraal, which we reached at nightfall. It is built on open ground, after the Zulu fashion, in a ring-fence, and with bee-hive huts. The cattle kraal is behind, and a little to the left. Indeed, both from their habits and their talk, it was easy to see that these Butiana belong to that section of the Bantu people which since T' Chaka's time has been known as the Zulu race. We did not see the chief Nala that night. His daughter Maiwa went on to his private huts as soon as we arrived, and very shortly afterwards one of his headmen came to us, bringing a sheep and some mealies and milk with him. 'The chief sent us greeting,' he said, and would see us on the morrow. Meanwhile he was ordered to bring us to a place of resting, where we and our goods should be safe and undisturbed. Accordingly he led the way to some very good huts just outside Nala's private enclosure, and here we slept comfortably.

"On the morrow about eight o'clock the headman came again, and said that Nala requested that I would visit him. Accordingly I followed him into the private enclosure, and was introduced to the chief — a fine-looking man of about fifty, with very delicately shaped hands and feet, and a rather nervous mouth. The chief was seated on a tanned ox-hide outside his hut. By his side was his daughter Maiwa, and round him, squatted on their haunches, were some twenty headmen or Indunas, whose number was continually added to by fresh arrivals. These men saluted me as I entered, and the chief rose and took my hand, ordering a stool to be brought for me to sit on. When this was done, he with much eloquence and native courtesy thanked me for protecting his daughter in the painful and dangerous circumstances in which she found herself placed, and also complimented me very highly upon what he was pleased to call the

bravery with which I had defended the pass
in the rocks. I answered in appropriate terms,
saying that it was to Maiwa herself that thanks
were due, for had it not been for her warning
and knowledge of the country we should not
have been here to-day, while as to the defence
of the pass, I was fighting for my life, and that
put heart into me.

"These courtesies being concluded, Nala
called upon his daughter Maiwa to tell her
tale to the headmen, and this she did most
simply and effectively. She reminded them
that she had gone as an unwilling bride to
Wambe; that no cattle had been paid for her,
because Wambe had threatened war if she was
not sent as a free gift. Since she had entered
the kraal of Wambe her days had been days
of heaviness, and her nights nights of weeping.
She had been beaten, she had been neglected,
and made to do the work of a low-born wife—
she, a chief's daughter. She had borne a child,
and this was the story of the child. Then,
amidst a dead silence, she told them the awful
tale which she had already narrated to me.
When she had finished, her hearers gave a loud
ejaculation. '*Ou!*' they said — '*ou*, Maiwa,
daughter of Nala!'

"'Ay,' she went on, with flashing eyes—

'ay, it is true. My mouth is as full of truth as a flower of honey, and for tears my eyes are like the dew upon the grass at dawn. It is true; I saw the child die. Here is the proof of it, Councillors;' and she drew forth the little dead hand, and held it before them.

"'*Ou!*' they said again—'*ou!* it is the dead hand.'

"'Yes,' she continued, 'it is the dead hand of my dead child, and I bear it with me that I may never forget, never for one short hour, that I may see Wambe die and be avenged. Will you bear with it, my father, that your daughter and your daughter's child should be so treated by a Matuku. Will ye bear it, men of my own people?'

"'No,' said an old Induna, rising; 'it is not to be borne. Enough have we suffered at the hands of these Matuku dogs and their loud-tongued chief. Let us put it to the issue.'

"'It is not to be borne indeed,' said Nala; 'but how can we make head against so great a people?'

"'Ask of him—ask of Macumazahn the wise white man,' said Maiwa, pointing to me.

"'How can we overcome Wambe, Macumazahn the hunter?'

" ' How does the jackal overreach the lion, Nala ?'

" ' By cleverness, Macumazahn.'

" ' So shall you overcome Wambe, Nala.'

" At this moment an interruption occurred. A man entered, and said that messengers had arrived from Wambe.

" ' What is their message ?' asked Nala.

" ' They come to ask that thy daughter Maiwa be sent back, and with her the white hunter.'

" ' How shall I make answer to this, Macumazahn ?' said Nala, when the man had withdrawn.

" ' Thus shalt thou answer,' I said, after reflection. ' Say that the woman shall be sent and I with her, and then bid the messengers begone. Stay; I will hide myself here in the hut that the men may not see me.' And I did.

" Shortly afterwards, through a crack in the hut, I saw the messengers arrive, and great truculent - looking fellows they were. There were four of them, and they had evidently travelled hard. They entered with a swagger, and squatted down before Nala.

" ' Your business ?' said Nala, frowning.

" ' We come from Wambe, bearing the or-

ders of Wambe to Nala his servant,' answered
the spokesman of the party.

"'Speak,' said Nala, with a curious twitch
of his nervous-looking mouth.

"'These are the words of Wambe, "Send
back the woman, my wife, who has run away
from my kraal, and send with her the white
man who has dared to hunt in my country
without my leave, and to slay my soldiers."
These are the words of Wambe.'

"'And if I say I will not send them?' asked
Nala.

"'Then, on behalf of Wambe, we declare
war upon you. Wambe will eat you up. He
will wipe you out. Your kraals shall be
stamped flat—so;' and with an expressive gest-
ure he drew his hand across his mouth to show
how complete would be the annihilation of the
chief who dared to defy Wambe.

"'These are heavy words,' said Nala. 'Let
me think before I give an answer.'

"Then followed a little piece of acting that
was really very creditable to the untutored
savage mind. The heralds withdrew, but not
out of sight, and Nala went through the show
of earnestly consulting his Indunas. The girl
Maiwa, too, flung herself at his feet, and appeared to weep and implore his protection,

while he wrung his hands as though in doubt
and tribulation of mind. At length he summoned the messengers to draw near and ad-
dressed them, while Maiwa sobbed very realis-
tically at his side.

" ' Wambe is a great chief,' said Nala, ' and
this woman is his wife, whom he has a right to
claim. She must return to him, but her feet
are sore with walking ; she cannot come now.
In eight days from this day she shall be delivered at the kraal of Wambe; I will send her
with a party of my men. As for the white
hunter and his men, I have naught to do with
them, and cannot answer for their misdeeds.
They have wandered hither unasked by me,
and I will deliver them back whence they
came, that Wambe may judge them according
to his law. They shall be sent with the girl.
For you, go your ways. Food shall be given
you without the kraal, and a present for Wambe in atonement of the ill-doing of my daughter. I have spoken.'

" At first the heralds seemed inclined to insist upon Maiwa's accompanying them then
and there, but ultimately, on being shown the
swollen condition of her feet, they gave up the
point and departed.

" When they were well out of the way I

emerged from the hut, and we went on to discuss the situation and make our plans. First of all, as I was careful to explain to Nala, I was not going to give him my experience and services for nothing. I heard that Wambe had a stockade round his kraal made of elephant tusks. These tusks, in the event of our succeeding in our enterprise, I should claim as my perquisite, with the proviso that Nala should furnish me with men to carry them down to the coast.

"To this modest request he and the headmen gave an unqualified and hearty assent, the more hearty, perhaps, because they never expected to finger them.

"The next thing that I stipulated was that, if we conquered, the white man John Every should be handed over to me, together with any goods that he might claim. His cruel captivity was, I need hardly say, the only reason that induced me to join in so hare-brained an expedition; but I was careful, from motives of policy, to keep this fact in the background. Nala accepted this condition. My third stipulation was that no women or children should be killed. This being also agreed to, we went on to consider ways and means. Wambe was, it appeared, a very powerful petty chief; that

is, he could put at least six thousand fighting-
men into the field, and always had from three to
four thousand collected about his kraal, which
was supposed to be impregnable. Nala, on the
contrary, could not, at such short notice, collect more than from a thousand to twelve hundred men, though, being of the Zulu stock,
they were of much better stuff for fighting
purposes than Wambe's Matukus.

"These odds, though large, were not, under
the circumstances, overwhelming. The real
obstacle to our chance of success was the difficulty of delivering a crushing assault against
Wambe's strong place. This was, it appeared,
fortified all round with schanses, or stone
walls, and contained numerous caves and koppies in the hill-side and at the foot of the
mountain which no force had ever been able
to capture. It was said that in the time of
the Zulu monarch, Dingaan, a great impi of
that king's, having penetrated to this district,
had delivered an assault upon the kraal, then
owned by a forefather of Wambe's, and been
beaten back, with the loss of more than a
thousand men. Having thought the question
over, I closely interrogated Maiwa as to the
fortifications and the topographical peculiari-
ties of the spot, and not without results. I

discovered that the kraal was indeed impregnable to a front attack, but that it was very
slightly defended to the rear, which ran up
the slope of the mountain: indeed, only by
two lines of stone walls. The reason of this
was that the mountain is quite impassable, except by one secret path, supposed to be known
only to the chief and his councillors, and this
being so, it had not been considered necessary
to fortify it.

"'Well,' I said, when she had done, 'and
now as to this secret path of thine, knowest
thou aught of it ?'

"'Ay,' she answered; 'I am no fool, Macumazahn. Knowledge learned is power earned.
I won the secret of that path.'

"'And canst thou guide an impi thereon, so
that it shall fall upon the town from behind ?'

"'Yes, this can I do, if only Wambe's people know not that the impi comes, for if they
know then can they block the way.'

"'So, then, here is my plan. Listen, Nala,
and say if it be good, or if you have a better
show it forth. Let messengers go out and
summon all thy impi, that it be gathered here
on the third day from now. This being done,
let the impi, led by Maiwa, march on the morrow of the fourth day, and, crossing the moun-

tains, let it travel along on the other side of
the mountains till it come to the place on the
farther side of which is the kraal of Wambe;
that shall be some three days' journey in all
(about one hundred and twenty miles). Then,
on the night of the third day's journey, let
Maiwa lead the impi in silence up the secret
path, so that it comes to the crest of the mountain that is above the Strong Place, and here
let it hide among the rocks. Meanwhile, on
the sixth day from now, let one of the Indunas
of Nala bring with him two hundred men that
have guns, and take me and my men as prisoners, and take also a girl from among the Butiana people who by form and face is like unto
Maiwa, and bind her hands, and pass by the
road on which we came, and through the cutting in the cliff, on to the kraal of Wambe.
But the men shall take no shields or plumes
with them, only their guns and one short spear,
and when they meet the people of Wambe, they
shall say that they come to give up the woman
and the white man and his party to Wambe,
and to make atonement to Wambe. So shall
they pass in peace, and travelling thus, on the
evening of the seventh day we shall come to
the gates of the place of Wambe, and nigh the
gates there is, so says Maiwa, a koppie very

strong and full of rocks and caves, but having no soldiers thereon except in time of war, or, at the worst, but a few such as can easily be overpowered.

" 'This being done at the dawn of day, must the impi on the mountain behind the town light a fire and put wet grass thereon, so that the smoke goes up. Then at the sight of the smoke will we in the koppie begin to shoot into the town of Wambe, whereon all the soldiers will run to kill us. But we will hold our own, and while we fight the impi shall charge down the mountain-side and climb the schanses, and put those who defend them to the assegai, and then, falling upon the town, shall surprise it, and drive the soldiers of Wambe as the wind blows the dead husks of corn. This is my plan. I have spoken.'

" '*Ou,*' said Nala, 'it is good; it is very good. The white man is cleverer than a jackal. Yes, so shall it be, and may the Snake of the Butiana people stand up upon its tail and prosper the war, for so shall we be rid of Wambe, and the tyrannies of Wambe.'

"After that the girl Maiwa stood up, and once more producing the dreadful little dried hand, made her father and several of his head councillors swear by it and upon it that they

would carry out the war of vengeance to the
bitter end. It was a very curious sight to see,
and the fight that ensued was, by the way,
thereafter known among the tribes of that
district as the War of the Little Hand.

"The next two days were busy ones for us.
Messengers were sent out, and every available
man of the Butiana tribe was ordered up to 'a
great dance.' The country was small, and by
the evening of the second day some twelve
hundred and fifty men were assembled, with
their assegais and shields, and a fine, hardy
troop they were.

"At dawn of the following day, the fourth
from the departure of the heralds, the main impi
started, under the command of Nala himself,
who, knowing that his life and chieftainship
hung upon the issue of the struggle, wisely determined to be present to direct it. With them
went Maiwa, who was to guide them up the secret path. Of course he had to give them two
days' start, as they had more than a hundred
miles of rough country to pass, including the
crossing of the great mountain-range which ran
north and south, for it was necessary that the
impi should make a wide detour in order to escape detection. At length, however, at dawn on
the sixth day, I took the road, accompanied by

my most unwilling bearers, who did not at all
like the idea of thus putting their heads into
the lion's mouth. Indeed, it was only the fear
of Nala's spears, together with a vague confidence in myself, that induced them to accept
the adventure. With me also were about two
hundred Butianas, all armed with guns of
various kinds, for many of these people had
guns, though they were not very proficient in
the use of them. But they carried no shield,
and wore no head-dress or armlets; indeed,
every warlike appearance was carefully avoided. With our party went also a sister of Maiwa's, though by a different mother, who strongly resembled her in face and form, and whose
mission it was to personate the runaway wife.

"That evening we camped upon the top of
the cliff up which we had so barely escaped, and
next morning at the first breaking of the light
we rolled away the stones with which we had
blocked the passage some days before, and descended to the hill-side beneath. Here the
bodies, or rather the skeletons, of the men who
had fallen before my rifle still lay about. The
Matuku soldiers had left their comrades to be
buried by the vultures. I descended the gully
into which poor Gobo had fallen, and searched
for his body, but in vain, although I found the

spot where he and the other man had struck, together with the bones of the latter, which I recognized by the waist-cloth. Either some beast of prey had carried Gobo off, or the Matuku people had disposed of his remains, and also of my express rifle which he carried. At any rate, I never saw or heard any more of him.

"Once in Wambè's country, we adopted a very circumspect method of proceeding. About fifty men marched ahead, in loose order, to guard against surprise, while as many more followed behind. The other hundred were gathered in a bunch between, and in the centre of these men I marched, together with the girl who was personating Maiwa and all my bearers. We were disarmed, and some of my men were tied together, to show that we were prisoners, while the girl had a blanket thrown over her head, and moved along with an air of great dejection. We headed straight for Wambè's place, which was at a distance of about twenty-five miles from the mountain-pass.

"When we had gone some five miles we met a party of about fifty of Wambè's soldiers, who were evidently on the lookout for us. They stopped us, and their captain asked where we were going. The headman of our party answered that he was conveying Mai-

wa, Wambe's runaway wife, together with the
white hunter and his men, to be given up to
Wambe, in accordance with his command.
The captain then wanted to know why we
were so many, to which our spokesman replied that I and my men were very desperate
fellows, and that it was feared that if we were
sent with a smaller escort we should escape,
and bring disgrace and the wrath of Wambe
upon their tribe. Thereon this gentleman, the
Matuku captain, began to amuse himself at my
expense, and mock me, saying that Wambe
would make me pay for the soldiers that I
had killed. He would put me into the ' Thing
that bites '—in other words, the lion trap—and
leave me there to die like a jackal caught by
the leg. I made no answer to this, though my
wrath was great, but pretended to be frightened. Indeed, there was not much pretence
about it—I was frightened. I could not con-
ceal from myself that ours was a most hazard-
ous enterprise, and that it was very possible
that I might make acquaintance with that lion
trap before I was many days older. However,
it was quite impossible to desert poor Every in
his misfortune, so I had to go on, and trust to
Providence, as I have so often had to do before and since.

" And now a fresh difficulty arose. Wambe's
soldiers insisted upon accompanying us, and,
what is more, did all they could to urge us forward, as they were naturally anxious to get to
the chief's place before evening. But we, on
the other hand, had excellent reasons for not
arriving till night was closing in, since we re-
lied upon the gloom to cover our advance upon
the koppie which commanded the town. Fi-
nally they got so importunate that we had to
flatly refuse to move faster, alleging as a reason that the girl was tired. They did not accept this excuse in good part, and at one time
I thought that we should have come to blows,
for there is no love lost between Butianas and
Matukus. At last, however, either from motives of policy or because they were so evidently outnumbered, they gave in, and suffered us
to go our own pace. I earnestly wished that
they would have added to the obligation by
going theirs, but this they absolutely declined
to do. On the contrary, they accompanied us
every foot of the way, keeping up a running
fire of allusions to the ' Thing that bites ' that
jarred upon my nerves and discomposed my
temper.

" About half-past four in the afternoon we
came to a neck or ridge of stony ground,

whence we could plainly see Wambe's town, lying some six or seven miles away, and three thousand feet beneath us. The town is built in a valley, with the exception of Wambe's own kraal; that is situated at the mouth of some caves upon the slope of the opposing mountains, over which I hoped to see our impi's spears come flashing in the morrow's light. Even from where we stood it was easy to see how strongly the place was fortified with schanses and stone walls, and how difficult of approach. Indeed, unless taken by surprise, it seemed to me quite impregnable to a force operating without cannon, and even cannon would not make much impression on rocks and stony koppies filled with caves.

" Then came the descent of the pass, and an arduous business it was, for the path—if it may be called a path—was almost entirely composed of huge water-worn boulders, from the one to the other of which we had to jump like so many grasshoppers. It took us two hours to get down; and travelling through that burning sun, when at last we did reach the bottom, I, for one, was pretty nearly played out. Shortly afterwards, just as it was growing dark, we came to the first line of fortifications, which consisted of a triple stone wall pierced by a gateway so narrow that a man could hardly squeeze through it. We passed this without question, being accompanied by Wambe's soldiers. Then came a belt of land three hundred paces or more in width, very rocky and broken, and having no huts upon it. It was in hollows in this belt that the cattle were kraaled in case of danger. On the farther side were more fortifications, and another small gateway shaped like an inverted V, and just beyond and through it I saw the koppie we had planned to seize looming up against the line of mountains behind. As we went I whispered my suggestions to our captain, with the result that at the second gateway he halted the cavalcade, and, addressing the captain of Wambe's soldiers, said that we would wait here till we received Wambe's word to enter the town.

"The other man said that that was well, only he must hand over the prisoners to be taken up to the chief's kraal, for Wambe was 'hungry to begin upon them,' and his 'heart desired to see the white man at rest before he closed his eyes in sleep;' and as for his wife, surely he would welcome her. Our leader replied that he could not do this thing, because his orders were to deliver the prisoners to Wambe at Wambe's own kraal, and they might not be broken. How could he be responsible for the safety of the prisoners if he let them out of his hand? No; they would wait there till Wambe's word was brought.

"To this, after some demur, the other man consented, and departed, remarking· that he would soon be back. As he passed me he called out, with a sneer, pointing, as he did, to the fading red in the western sky, ' Look your last upon the light, white man, for the " Thing that bites " lives in the dark.'

"Next day it so happened that I shot this man, and, do you know, I think that he is about the only human being who has come to harm at my hands for whom I do not feel sincere sorrow and, in a degree, remorse.

CHAPTER VII.

THE ATTACK.

" Just where we halted ran a little stream of water. I looked at it, and an idea struck me. Probably there would be no water on the koppie. I suggested this to our captain, and acting on the hint, he directed all the men to drink what they could, and also to fill the seven or eight cooking-pots which we had with us with water. Then came the crucial moment. How were we to get possession of the koppie? When our captain asked me, I said that I thought we had better march up and take it, and this accordingly we went on to do. When we came to the narrow gateway, we were, as I expected, stopped by two soldiers who were on guard there, and asked our business. The captain answered that we had changed our mind, and would follow on to Wambe's kraal. The soldiers said no; we must now wait.

" To this we replied by pushing them to one

side, and marching in single file through the gateway, which was not distant more than a hundred yards from the koppie. While we were getting through, the men we had pushed away ran towards the town, calling for assistance—a call that was promptly responded to, for in another minute we made out scores of armed men running hard in our direction. So we ran too, for the koppie. As soon as they understood what we were after, which they did not at first, owing to the dimness of the light, they did their level best to get to the koppie before us. But we had the start of them, and with the exception of one unfortunate man, who stumbled and fell, we were well on to it before they arrived. This man they captured, and when fighting began on the following morning, and he refused to give any information, they killed him. Luckily they had no time to torture him, or they would certainly have done so, for these Matuku people are very fond of torturing their enemies.

"When we reached the koppie, the base of which covered about half an acre of ground, the soldiers who had been trying to cut us off halted, for they knew the strength of the position. This gave us a few minutes, before the light had quite vanished, to reconnoitre the place.

We found that it was unoccupied, fortified
with a regular labyrinth of stone walls, and
contained three large caves and some smaller
ones.   The next business was to post the men
to such advantage as time would allow.   My
own men I was careful to put right at the top.
They were perfectly useless from terror, and
what I feared was that they might try to escape and give information of our plans to
Wambe.   So I watched them like the apple
of my eye, telling them that should they dare
to stir they would be shot.

" Then it grew quite dark, and presently
out of the darkness I heard a voice; it was
that of the leader of the soldiers who had es-
corted us, calling to us to come down.   We
replied that it was too dark to move; we
should hit our feet against the stones.   He
insisted upon our descending, and we flatly refused, saying that if any attempt was made
to dislodge us we would fire.   After that, as
they had no real intention of attacking us in
the dark, the men withdrew, but we saw from
the watch-fires that were lit around that they
were keeping a strict watch upon our position.

" That night was a wearing one, for we
never quite knew how the situation was going
to develop.   Fortunately we had some cooked

food with us, so we did not starve. It was, however, lucky that we had drunk our fill before coming up, for, as I had anticipated, there was not a drop of water on the koppie.

" At length the night wore away, and with the first tinge of light I began to go my rounds, and, stumbling along the stony paths, make things as ready as I could for the attack, which I felt sure would be delivered before we were two hours older. The men were cramped and cold, and consequently low-spirited, but I exhorted them to the best of my ability, bidding them remember the race from which they sprang, and not show the white feather to a crowd of Matuku dogs. At length it began to grow light, and presently I saw long columns of men advancing towards the koppie. They halted, under cover, at a distance of about a hundred and fifty yards, and just as the dawn broke a herald came forward and called to us. Our captain stood up on a rock and answered him.

" ' These are the words of Wambe,' he said. ' Come forth from the koppie and give over the evil-doers, and go in peace, or stay on the koppie and be slain.'

" ' It is too early to come forth as yet,' answered our man, in fine diplomatic style.

'When the sun sucks up the mist, then will we come forth.   Our limbs are stiff with cold.'

" ' Come forth even now,' said the herald.

" ' Not if I know it, my boy,' said I to my-self; but the captain replied that he would come out when he thought proper, and not before.

" ' Then make ready to die,' said the herald; for all the world like the villain of a transpon-tine piece, and stalked majestically back to the soldiers.

" I made my final arrangements, and looked anxiously at the mountain crest, a couple of miles or so away, from which the mist was now beginning to lift, but no column of smoke could I see.   I whistled, for if the attacking force had been delayed or made any mistake, our position was likely to grow pretty warm. We had barely enough water to wet the mouths of the men, and when once that was finished we could not hold the place for long in the burning sun.

" At length, just as the sun rose in glory over the heights behind us, the Matuku sol-diers, of whom some fifteen hundred were now assembled, set up a queer whistling noise, which ended in a chant.   Next some shots were fired (for the Matuku had a few guns), but without effect, though one bullet passed just by a man's head. 'Now they are going to begin,' I thought to myself, and I was not far wrong, for in another minute the body of men divided into three companies, each about five hundred strong, and, heralded by a running fire, charged at us on three sides. Our men were now all well under cover, and the fire did us no harm. I mounted on a rock, so as to command a view of as much of the koppie and plain as possible, and yelled to our men to reserve their fire till I gave the word, and then to shoot low, and load as quickly as possible. I knew that, like all natives, they were sure to be execrable shots, and that they were armed with weapons made out of old gas-pipes, so the only chance of doing execution was to let the enemy get right on to us.

"On they came with a rush. They were within eighty yards now, and as they drew near the point of attack, I observed that they closed their ranks, which was so much the better for us.

"'Shall we not fire, my father?' sung out the captain.

"'No—confound you!' I answered.

"Sixty yards—fifty—forty—thirty. 'Fire, you scoundrels!' I yelled, setting the example by letting off both barrels of my elephant gun into the thickest part of the company opposite to me.

"Instantly the place rang with the discharge of two hundred and odd guns, while the air was torn by the passage of every sort of missile, from iron pot-legs down to slugs and pebbles coated with lead. The result was very prompt. The Matukus were so near that we could not miss them, and at thirty yards a lead-coated stone out of a gas-pipe is as effective as a Martini rifle, or more so. Over rolled the attacking soldiers by the dozen, while the survivors, fairly frightened, took to their heels. We plied them with shot till they were out of range ; I made it very warm for them with the elephant gun by the way, and then we loaded up in quite a cheerful frame of mind, for we had not lost a man, whereas I could count more than fifty dead and wounded Matukus. The only thing that damped my ardor was that, stare as I would, I could see no column of smoke upon the mountain-crest.

" Half an hour elapsed before any further steps were taken against us. Then the attacking force adopted different tactics. Seeing that it was very risky to try to rush on us in dense masses, they opened out into skirmishing order, and ran across the open space in lots of five and six. As it happened, right at the foot of the koppie the ground broke away a little in such fashion that it was almost impossible for us to search it effectually with our fire. On the hither side of this dip Wambe's soldiers were now congregating in considerable numbers. Of course we did them as much damage as we could while they were running across, but this sort of work requires good shots, and that was just what we had not got. Another thing was that so many of our men would insist upon letting off the things they called guns at every little knot of the enemy that ran across. Thus the first few lots were indeed practically swept away, but after that, as it took a long while to load the gas-pipes and old flint muskets, those who followed got across in comparative safety. For my own part, I fired away with the elephant gun and repeating carbine till they grew almost too hot to hold, but my individual efforts could do nothing to stop such a rush, or perceptibly lessen the number of our enemies. At length there were at least a thousand men crowded into the dip of the ground within a few yards of us, whence those of them who had guns kept up a continued fusillade upon the koppie.

They killed two of my bearers in this way and
wounded a third, for being at the top of the
koppie, these men were most exposed to the
fire from the dip at its base.   Seeing that the
situation was growing most serious, I at length,
by the dint of threats and entreaties, persuaded the majority of our people to cease firing
useless shots, to reload and prepare for the rush.
Scarcely had I done so when the enemy came
for us with a roar.   I am bound to say that I
should never have believed that Matukus had
it in them to make such a determined charge.
A large party rushed round the base of the
koppie and attacked us in flank, while the
others swarmed wherever they could get a
foothold, so that we were taken on every side.

"'*Fire !*' I cried ; and we did, with terrible
effect.   Many of their men fell, but though we
checked, we could not stop them.   They closed
up, and rushed the first fortification, killing a
good number of its defenders.   It was almost
all cold steel work now, for we had no time to
reload, and that suited the Butiana habits of
fighting well enough, for the stabbing assegai
was a weapon which they understood.   Those
of our people who escaped from the first line
of walls took refuge in the second, where I
stood myself, encouraging them, and here the

fight raged fiercely. Occasionally parties of
the enemy would force a passage, only to per-
ish on the hither side beneath the Butiana
spears. But still they kept it up, and I saw
that, fight as we would, we were doomed. We
were altogether outnumbered, and, to make
matters worse, fresh bodies of soldiers were
pouring across the plain to the assistance of
our assailants. So I made up my mind to
direct a retreat into the caves, and there expire
in a manner as heroic as circumstances would
allow, and while mentally lamenting my hard
fate, and reflecting on my sins, I fought away
like a fiend. It was then I remember that
I shot my friend the captain of our escort of
the previous day. He had caught sight of me,
and making a vicious dig at my stomach with
a spear (which I successfully dodged) shouted
out, or rather began to shout out, one of his
unpleasant allusions to the ' Thing that—' He
never got as far as ' bites,' because I shot him
after ' that.'

" Well, the game was about up. Already I
saw one man throw down his spear in token of
surrender, which act of cowardice cost him his
life, by the way, when suddenly a shout arose.

" ' Look at the mountain !' they cried ; ' there
is an impi on the mountain-side.'

" I glanced up, and there, sure enough, about
half-way down the mountain, nearing the first
fortification, the long-plumed double line of
Nala's warriors were rushing down to battle,
the bright light of the morning glancing on
their spears. Afterwards we discovered that
the reason of their delay was that they had
been stopped by a river in flood, and could not
reach the mountain-crest by dawn. When they
did reach it, however, they instantly saw that
the fight was already going on—was ' in flower,' as they put it—and so advanced at once
without waiting to light fires.

" Meanwhile they had been observed from
the town, and parties of soldiers were charging up the steep side of the hill to occupy the
schanses and the second line of fortifications
behind them. The first line they did not now
attempt to reach or defend : Nala pressed them
too close. But they got to the schanses or pits
protected with stone walls, and constructed to
hold from a dozen to twenty men, and soon
began to open fire from them and from isolated
rocks. I turned my eyes to the gates of the
town, which were placed to the north and
south. Already they were crowded with hundreds of fugitive women and children flying
to the rocks and caves for shelter from the foe.

As for ourselves, the appearance of Nala's impi
produced a wonderful change for the better in
our position. The soldiers attacking us, realiz-
ing that the town was being assailed from the
rear, simply turned, and, clambering down the
koppie, streamed off to protect their homes
against this new enemy. In five minutes there
was not a man left except those who would
move no more, or were too sorely wounded to
escape. I felt inclined to ejaculate ' *Saved !*'
like the gentleman in the play, but did not,
because the occasion was too serious. What I
did do was to muster all the men and reckon
up our losses. They amounted to fifty-one
killed and wounded, sixteen men having been
killed outright. Then I sent men with the
cooking-pots to the stream for water, and we
drank. This done, I set my bearers, as being
the most useless part of the community from
a fighting point of view, to the task of attending the injured, and turned to watch the fray.

" By this time Nala's impi had climbed the
first line of fortifications without opposition,
and were advancing in a long line upon the
schanses or pits which were scattered about
between it and the second line, singing a war
chant as they came. Presently puffs of smoke
began to start from the schanses, and with my

glasses I could see several of our men falling
over. Then, as they came opposite a schanse,
that portion of the long line of warriors would
thicken up and charge it with a wild rush. I
could clearly see them leap on to the walls and
vanish into the depths beneath, some of their
number falling backward on each occasion, shot
or stabbed to death. Next would come another
act in the tragedy. Out from the hither side of
the schanse would pour such of its defenders as
were left alive, perhaps three or four, and perhaps a dozen, running for dear life, with the
war-dogs on their tracks. One by one they
would be caught, then up flashed the great
spear, and down fell the pursued, dead. I saw
ten of our men leap into one large schanse, but
though I watched for some time, nobody came
out. Afterwards we inspected the place, and
found these all dead, together with twenty-
three Matukus. Neither side would give in,
and they had fought it out to the bitter end.

"At last they neared the second line of fortifications, behind which the whole remaining
Matuku force, numbering some two thousand
men, was rapidly assembling. One little pause
to get their breath, and they came at it with
a rush, and a long wild shout of '*Bulala Matuku!*' (Kill the Matukus!) that went right

through me. Then came an answering shout
and the sounds of heavy firing, and presently
I saw our men retreating, somewhat fewer in
numbers than they had advanced. Their welcome had been a warm one, for the Matuku
fight splendidly behind walls.

"This decided me that it was necessary to cre-
ate a diversion. If we did not do so, it seemed
very probable that we should be worsted, after
all. I called to the captain of our little force,
and rapidly put the position before him. Seeing
the urgency of the occasion, he agreed with me
that we must risk it, and in two minutes more we
were, with the exception of my own men, whom
I left to guard the wounded, trotting across
the open space, and through the deserted town,
towards the spot where the struggle was taking place, some seven hundred yards away.
In seven or eight minutes we reached a group
of huts—it was a headman's kraal, that was
situated about a hundred and twenty yards
behind the fortified wall, and took possession
of it unobserved. The enemy was too much
engaged with the foe in front of them to notice
us, and, besides, the broken ground rose in a
hog-back shape between. There we waited a
minute or two and recovered our breath, while
I gave my directions. So soon as we heard

the Butiani impi begin to charge again, we
were to run out in line to the brow of the hog-
back, and pour our fire into the mass of the
defenders behind the wall.   Then the guns
were to be thrown down, and we must charge
with the assegai.   We had no shields, but that
could not be helped ; there would be no time to
reload the guns, and it was absolutely necessary
that the enemy should be disconcerted at the
moment that the main attack was delivered.

"The men, who were as plucky a set of
fellows as ever I saw, and whose blood was
now thoroughly up, consented to this scheme,
though I could see that they thought it rather
a large order, as indeed I did myself.   But I
knew that if the impi was driven back a second
time the game would be up, and for me, at any
rate, it would be a case of the 'Thing that
bites,' and this sure and certain knowledge
filled my breast with valor.

"We had not long to wait.   Presently we
heard the Butiana war-song swelling loud and
long.   They had commenced their attack.   I
made a sign, and the hundred and fifty men,
headed by myself, poured out of the kraal, and,
getting into a rough line, ran up the fifty or
sixty yards of slope that intervened between
ourselves and the crest of the hog-backed ridge.

In thirty seconds we were there, and immediately beyond us was the main body of the Matuku host waiting the onslaught of the enemy with guns and spears. Even now they did not see us, so intent were they upon the coming attack. I signed to my men to take careful aim, and suddenly called out to them to fire, which they did with a will, dropping thirty or forty Matukus.

" ' *Charge !*' I shouted again, throwing down my smoking rifle, and drawing my revolver, an example which they followed, snatching up their spears from the ground where they had placed them while they fired. The men set up a savage whoop, and we started. I saw the Matuku soldiers wheel round in hundreds, utterly taken aback at this new development of the situation. And looking over them, before we had gone twenty yards, I saw something else. For of a sudden, as though they had risen from the earth, there appeared above the wall hundreds of great spears, followed by hundreds of savage faces shadowed with drooping plumes. With a yell they sprang upon the wall, shaking their broad shields, and with a yell they bounded from it straight into our astonished foes.

" *Crash !* we were in them now, and fighting
Vol. 13—15

like demons. *Crash!* from the other side.
Nala's impi was at its work, and still the spears
and plumes appeared for a moment against
the brown background of the mountain, and
then sprang down and rushed like a storm
upon the foe. The great mob of men turned
this way and turned that way, astonished, be-
wildered, overborne by doubt and terror. Meanwhile the slayers stayed not their hands, and on
every side spears flashed, and the fierce shout
of triumph went up to heaven. There too, on
the wall, stood Maiwa, a white garment streaming from her shoulders, an assegai in her hand,
her breast heaving, her eyes flashing. Above
all the din of battle I could catch the tones of
her clear voice as she urged the soldiers on to
victory. But victory was not yet. Wambe's
soldiers gathered themselves together and bore
our men back by the sheer weight of numbers.
They began to give, then once more they ral-
lied and the fight hung doubtfully.

"'Slay, you war whelps!' cried Maiwa, from
the wall. 'Are you afraid, you women, you
chicken-hearted women? Strike home, or die
like dogs! What! you give way? Follow me,
children of Nala.' And with one wild, long cry,
she leaped from the wall as leaps a stricken
antelope, and, holding the spear poised on high,

rushed right into the thickest of the fray.
The warriors saw her, and raised such a shout
that it echoed like thunder against the mountains. They massed together, and, following
the flutter of her white robe, crashed into the
dense heart of the foe. Down went the Matuku before them like trees before a whirlwind.
Nothing could stand before such a rush as that.
It was as the rush of a torrent bursting its banks.
All along their line swept the wild, desperate
charge, and there, straight in the fore-front of
the battle, still waved the white robe of Maiwa.

" Then they broke, and, stricken with utter
panic, Wambe's soldiers streamed away, a scattered crowd of fugitives, while after them thundered the footfall of the victors.

" The fight was over; we had won the day;
and for my part I sat down upon a stone and
wiped my forehead, thanking Providence that
I had lived to see the end of it. Twenty minutes later Nala's warriors began to return,
panting. ' Wambe's soldiers had taken to the
bush and the caves,' they said, ' where they had
not thought it safe to follow them,' adding, sig-
nificantly, that many had stopped on the way.

" I was utterly dazed, and now that the fight
was over, my energy seemed to have left me,
and I did not pay much attention, till pres-

ently I was aroused by somebody calling me
by my name. I looked up, and saw that it
was the chief Nala himself, who was bleeding
from a flesh-wound in his arm. By his side
stood Maiwa, panting but unhurt, and wearing the same proud and terrifying air.

" ' They are gone, Macumazahn,' said the
chief; 'there is little to fear from them; their
heart is broken. But where is Wambe the chief,
and where is the white man thou camest to save?'

" ' I know not,' I answered.

" Close to where we stood lay a Matuku, a
young man who had been shot through the
fleshy part of the calf. It was a trifling wound,
but it prevented him from running away.

" ' Say, thou dog,' said Nala, stalking up to
him, and shaking his red spear in his face—
'say, where is Wambe! Speak, or I slay thee.
Was he with the soldiers?'

" ' Nay, lord, I know not,' groaned the terrified man. ' He fought not with us. Wambe
has no stomach for fighting. Perchance he is
in his kraal yonder, or in the cave behind the
kraal;' and he pointed to a small enclosure on
the hill-side about four hundred yards to the
right of where we were.

" ' Let us go and see,' said Nala, summoning
his soldiers.

CHAPTER VIII.

MAIWA IS AVENGED.

" THE impi formed up. Alas ! an hour before it had been stronger by a third than it
was now. Then Nala detached two hundred
men to collect and attend to the injured, and
at my suggestion issued a stringent order that
none of the enemy's wounded, and above all
no women or children, were to be killed, as is
the savage custom among African natives. On
the contrary, they were to be allowed to send
word to their women that they might come
in to nurse them, and fear nothing, for Nala
made war upon Wambe the tyrant, and not
on the Matuku tribe. Then we started with
some four hundred men for the chief's kraal.
Very soon we were there. It was, as I have
said, placed against the mountain - side, but
within the fortified lines, and did not cover
more than an acre and a half of ground altogether. Outside was a tidy reed fence, within
which, neatly arranged in a semicircular line,

stood the huts of the chief's principal wives.
Maiwa, of course, knew every inch of the kraal,
for she had lived in it, and led us straight to
the entrance. We peeped through the gateway. Not a soul was to be seen. There were
the huts, and there was the clear open space,
floored with a concrete of lime, on which the
sun beat fiercely, but nobody could we see or
hear.

"'The jackal has gone to earth,' said Maiwa.
'He will be in the cave behind his hut,' and
she pointed with her spear towards another
small and semicircular enclosure, over which
a large hut was visible, that had the cliff itself
for a background. I stared at this fence. By
George, it was true! it was entirely made of
tusks of ivory planted in the ground, with their
points bending outward. The smallest ones,
though none were small, were placed nearest
to the cliff on either side, but they gradually
increased in size till they culminated in two
enormous tusks, which set up so that their
points met something in the shape of an inverted V, forming the gateway to the hut. I
was dumfounded with delight, and, indeed,
where is the elephant-hunter who would not
be if he suddenly saw five or six hundred
picked tusks set up in a row, and only wait-

ing for him to take them away. Of course
the stuff was what is known as 'black' ivory;
that is, the exterior of the tusks had become
black from years, or, perhaps, centuries of ex-
posure to wind and weather, but I was certain that it would be none the worse for that.
Forgetting the danger of the proceeding, I
actually ran, in my excitement, right across the
open space, and, drawing my knife, scratched
vigorously at one of the great tusks to see
how deep the damage was. As I thought, it
was nothing; there beneath the black covering gleamed the pure white ivory. I could
have capered for joy, for I fear that I am very
mercenary at heart, when suddenly I heard
the faint echo of a cry for assistance. ' Help!'
screamed a voice in the Sisutu dialect from
somewhere beyond the hut—'help! they are
murdering me.'

"*I knew the voice.* It was John Every's.
Oh, what a selfish brute was I! for the moment that miserable ivory had driven the recollection of him out of my head, and now
perhaps it was too late.

"Nala, Maiwa, and the soldiers had now
come up. They, too, had heard the voice,
and interpreted its tone, though they had not
caught the words.

" ' This way !' cried Maiwa ; and we started
at a run, passing round the hut of Wambe.
Behind was the narrow entrance to a cave.
We rushed through it, heedless of the danger
of an ambush, and this was what we saw,
though very confusedly at first, owing to the
gloom :

" In the centre of the cave and with either
end secured to the floor by strong stakes, was
a huge double-springed lion trap fringed with
sharp and grinning teeth. It was set, and beyond the trap, indeed almost over it, a terrible struggle was in progress. A naked, or
almost naked white man, with a great beard
hanging down over his breast, was, in spite of
his furious struggles, being slowly forced and
dragged towards the trap by six or eight
women. Only one man was present, a fat,
cruel-looking man, with small eyes and a hanging lip. It was the chief Wambe, and he stood
by the trap ready to force the victim down
upon it as soon as the women had dragged
him into the necessary position.

" At this instant they caught sight of us,
and there was a moment's pause ; and then,
before I knew what she was going to do, Maiwa lifted the assegai she still held, and whirled
it at Wambe's head. I saw the flash of light

speed towards him, and so did he, for he stepped backward to avoid it—stepped backward right into the trap. He yelled with pain as the iron teeth of the 'Thing that bites' sprang up like living things and fastened into him—such a yell I have not often heard. Now, at last, he tasted of the torture which he had inflicted upon so many, and though I trust I am a Christian, I cannot say that I felt sorry for him.

" The assegai sped on and struck one of the women who had hold of the unfortunate Every, piercing through her arm. This made her leave go—an example that the other women quickly followed, so that Every fell to the ground, where he lay gasping.

" ' Kill the witches!' roared Nala, in a voice of thunder, pointing to the group of women.

" ' Nay,' gasped Every ; ' spare them. He made them do it.' And he pointed to the human fiend in the trap. Then Maiwa waved her hand to us to fall back, for the moment of her vengeance was come. We did so, and she strode up to her lord, and, flinging the white robe from her, stood before him, her fierce, beautiful face fixed like stone.

" ' Who am I ?' she cried, in so terrible a voice that he ceased his yells. 'Am I that woman who was given to thee for wife, and

whose child thou slewest? Or am I a spirit
come to see thee die? What is this?' she went
on, drawing the withered baby hand from the
pouch at her side. ' Is it the hand of a babe,
and how came that hand to be thus alone?
What cut it off from the babe, and where is
the babe? Is it a hand, or is it the vision of
a hand that shall presently tear thy throat?
Where are thy soldiers, Wambe? Do they
sleep, and eat, and go forth to do thy bidding,
or are they perchance dead and scattered like
the winter leaves?'

"He groaned, and the fierce-eyed woman
went on: 'Art thou still a chief, Wambe? or
does another take thy town and power; and,
say, lord, what doest thou there, and what is
that slave's leglet upon thy knee? Is it a
dream, Wambe, great lord and chief, or'—and
she lifted her clinched hands and shook them
in his face—' hath a woman's vengeance found
thee out, and a woman's wit overmatched thy
tyrannous strength? and art thou about to
slowly die in torments horrible to think on,
oh, thou accursed murderer of little children?'
and with one wild scream she dashed the dead
hand of the child straight into his face, and
then fell senseless on the floor. As for the
demon in the trap, he shrank back as far as

its iron bounds would allow, his eyes starting
out of his head with pain and terror, and then
once more began to yell.

"The whole scene was more than I could
stand.

"'Nala,' I said, 'this must not go on. That
man is a fiend, but he must not be left to die
there. See thou to it.'

"'Nay,' answered Nala, 'let him taste of
the food wherewith he hath fed so many;
leave him till death shall find him.'

"'That will I not,' I answered. 'Let his
end be swift. See thou to it.'

"'As thou wilt, Macumazahn,' answered the
chief, with a shrug of the shoulders. 'First, let
the white man and Maiwa be brought forth.'

"So the soldiers came forward and carried
Every and the woman into the open air. As
the former was borne past his tormentor, the
fallen chief, so cowardly was his wicked heart,
actually prayed him to intercede for him, and
save him from a fate which, but for our provi-
dential appearance, would have been Every's
own.

"So we went away, and in another moment
one of the biggest villains on the earth trou-
bled it no more. Once in the fresh air, Every
quickly recovered. I looked at him, and hor-

ror and sorrow pierced me through to see such
a sight. His face was the face of a man of
sixty, though he was not yet forty, and his poor
body was cut to pieces with stripes and scars,
and other marks of the torments which Wambe
had for years amused himself with inflicting
on him.

"As soon as he recovered himself a little
he struggled on to his knees, burst into a par-
oxysm of weeping, and, clasping my legs with
his emaciated arms, would have actually kissed
my feet.

"'What are you about, old fellow?' I said,
for I am not accustomed to that sort of thing,
and it made me feel uncomfortable.

"'Oh, God bless you!' he moaned—'God
bless you! If only you knew what I have
gone through. And to think that you should
have come to help me, and at the risk of your
own life! Well, you were always a true friend
—yes, yes, a true friend.'

"'Bosh!' I answered, testily; 'I'm a trader,
and I came after that ivory,' and I pointed to
the stockade of tusks. 'Did you ever hear of
an elephant-hunter who would not have risked
his immortal soul for them, and much more
his carcass?'

"But he took no notice of my explanations,

and went on God-blessing me as hard as ever, till at last I bethought me that a nip of brandy, of which I had a flask full, might steady his nerves a bit. I gave it him, and was not disappointed in the result, for he brisked up wonderfully. Then I hunted about in Wambe's hut, and found a kaross for him to put over his poor bruised shoulders, and he was quite a man again.

" ' Now,' I said, ' why did the late lamented Wambe want to put you in that trap ?'

" ' Because, as soon as they heard that the fight was going against them, and that Maiwa was charging at the head of Nala's impi, one of the women told Wambe that she had seen me write something on some leaves and give them to Maiwa before she went away to purify herself. Then, of course, he guessed that I had had something to do with your seizing the koppie and holding it, while the impi rushed the place from the mountain, so he determined to torture me to death before help could come. Oh, heavens! what a mercy it is to hear English again !'

" ' How long have you been a prisoner here, Every ?' I asked.

" ' Six years and a bit, Quatermain; I have lost count of the odd months lately. I came up here with Major Aldey and three other gen

tlemen and forty bearers. That devil Wambe
ambushed us, and murdered the lot to get their
guns. They weren't much use to him when
he got them, being breech-loaders, for the
fools fired away all the ammunition in a month
or two. However, they are all in good order,
and hanging up in the hut there. They didn't
kill me because one of them saw me mending
a gun just before they attacked us, so they
kept me as a kind of armorer. Twice I tried
to make a bolt of it, but was caught each time.
Last time Wambe had me flogged very nearly
to death; you can see the scars upon my back.
Indeed, I should have died if it hadn't been
for the girl Maiwa, who nursed me by stealth.
He got that accursed lion trap among our
things also, and I suppose he has tortured between one and two hundred people to death
in it. It was his favorite amusement, and he
would go every day and sit and watch his victim till he died. Sometimes he would give
him food and water to keep him alive longer, telling him or her that he would let him
go if he lived till a certain day. But he
never did let them go. They all died there,
and I could show you their bones behind that
rock.'

"'The devil!' I said, grinding my teeth.

'I wish I hadn't interfered. I wish I had
left him to the same fate.'

"'Well, he got a taste of it, anyway,' said
Every. 'I'm glad he got a taste. There's justice in it, and now he's gone to hell, and I
hope there is another one ready for him there.
By Jove! I should like to have the setting of
it.'

"And so he talked on, and I sat and listened
to him, wondering how he had kept his reason
for so many years. But he didn't talk, as I
have written it, in good English. He spoke
very slowly, and as though he had got something in his mouth, continually using native
words, because the English ones had slipped
his memory.

"At last Nala came up and told us that food
was made ready, and thankful enough we were
to get it, I can tell you. After we had eaten
we held a consultation. Quite a thousand of
Wambe's soldiers were put *hors de combat*, but
at least two thousand remained hidden in the
bush and rocks, and these men, together with
those in the outlying kraals, were a source of
possible danger. The question arose, therefore, what was to be done: were they to be
followed or left alone? I waited till everybody had spoken, some giving one opinion and

some another, and then, being appealed to, I
gave mine. It was to the effect that Nala
should take a leaf out of the great Zulu T'Chaka's book, and incorporate the tribe, not de-
stroy it. We had a good many women among
the prisoners. Let them, I suggested, be sent
to the hiding-places of the soldiers and make
an offer. If the men would come and lay
down their arms and declare their allegiance
to Nala, they and their town and cattle should
be spared. Wambe's cattle alone would be
seized as the prize of war. Moreover, Wambe
having left no children, his wife, Maiwa, should
be declared chieftainess of the tribe, under
Nala. If they did not accept this offer by the
morning of the second day, it should be taken
as a declaration that they wished to continue
the war. Their town should be burned, their
cattle, which our men were already collecting
and driving in in great numbers, would be
taken, and they should be hunted down.

"This advice was at once declared to be
wise, and acted on. The women were de-
patched, and I saw from their faces that they
never expected to get such terms, and did not
think that their mission would be in vain.
Nevertheless we spent that afternoon in preparations against possible surprise, and also in

collecting all the wounded of both parties into a hospital which we extemporized out of some huts, and there attending to them as best we could. That evening poor Every had the first pipe of tobacco that he had tasted for six years. Poor fellow! he nearly cried with joy over it. The night passed without any sign of attack, and on the following morning we began to see the effect of our message, for women, children, and a few men came in in little knots, and took possession of their huts. It was, of course, rather difficult to prevent our men from looting, and generally going on as natives, and, for the matter of that, white men too, are in the habit of doing after a victory. But one man, who, after warning, was caught maltreating a woman, was brought out and killed by Nala's order, and though there was a little grumbling, that put a stop to further trouble.

"On the second morning the headmen and numbers of their followers came in in groups, and about midday a deputation of the former presented themselves before us without their weapons. They were conquered, they said, and Wambe was dead, so they came to hear the words of the great lion who had eaten them up, and of the crafty white man, the jackal who had dug a hole for them to fall in,

and of Maiwa, Lady of War, who had led the
charge and turned the fate of the battle.

"So we let them hear the words; and when
we had done, an old man rose and said that
in the name of the people he accepted the
yoke that was laid upon their shoulders, and
that the more gladly because even the rule of
a woman could not be worse than the rule of
Wambe. Moreover, they knew Maiwa, the
Lady of War, and feared her not, though she
was a witch, and terrible to see in battle.

"Then Nala asked his daughter if she was
willing to become chieftainess of the tribe under him.

"Maiwa, who had been very silent since her
revenge was accomplished, answered yes, that
she was, and that her rule should be good and
gentle to those who were good and gentle to
her, but the froward and rebellious she would
smite with a rod of iron, which, from my
knowledge of her character, I thought ex-
ceedingly probable.

"The headmen replied that that was a good
saying, and they did not complain of it, and
so the meeting ended.

"Next day we spent in preparations for departure. Mine consisted chiefly in superin-
tending the digging up of the stockade of

ivory tusks, which I did with the greatest satisfaction. There were some five hundred of
them altogether. I made inquiries about it
from Every, who told me that the stockade
had been there so long that nobody seemed to
exactly know who had originally collected the
tusks. There was, however, a kind of super-
stitious feeling about them, which had always
prevented the chiefs from trying to sell this
great mass of ivory. Every and I examined
it carefully, and found that although it was
so old, its quality was really as good as ever,
and there was very little soft ivory in the lot.
At first I was rather afraid lest now that my
services had been rendered, Nala should hesitate to part with so much valuable property;
but this was not the case. When I spoke to
him on the subject he merely said, 'Take it,
Macumazahn, take it—you have earned it well.'
And to speak the truth, though I say it who
shouldn't, I think I had. So we pressed several hundred Matuku bearers into our service,
and next day marched off with the lot.

"Before we went I took a formal farewell
of Maiwa, whom we left with a bodyguard
of three hundred men to assist her in settling
the country. She gave me her hand to kiss
in a queenly sort of way, and then said: 'Ma-

cumazahn, you are a brave man, and have been
a good friend to me in my need. If ever you
want help or shelter, remember that Maiwa
has a good memory for friend and foe. All I
have is yours.'

"And so I thanked her, and went. She
certainly was a very remarkable woman. A
year or two ago I heard that her father Nala
was dead, and that she had succeeded to the
chieftainship of both tribes, which she ruled
with great justice and firmness.

"I can assure you that we ascended the pass
leading to Wambe's town with feelings very
different from those with which we had descended it a few days before. But if I was
grateful for the issue of events, you can easily imagine what poor Every's feelings were.
When we got to the top of the pass he actually, before the whole impi, flopped down upon
his knees and thanked Heaven for his escape,
with the tears running down his face. But
then, as I have said, his nerves were shaken;
though now that his beard was trimmed, and
he had got some sort of clothes on his back,
and hope in his heart, he looked a very different man from the poor wretch whom we had
rescued from death by torture.

"Well, we separated from Nala at the little

stairway, or pass, over the mountain. Every
and I and the ivory going down the river
which we had come up a few weeks before,
and the chief returning to his own kraal on
the farther side of the mountain. He gave us
an escort of a hundred and fifty men, however, with instructions to accompany us for six
days' journey, and keep the Matuku bearers in
order, and then return. I knew that in six
days we should be able to reach a district where
porters were plentiful, and whence we could
easily get the ivory conveyed to Delagoa Bay."

"And did you land it up safe?" I asked.

"Well, no," said Quatermain; "we lost
about a third of it in crossing a river. A
flood came down suddenly, just as the men
were crossing, and many of them had to throw
down their tusks to save their lives. We had
no means of fishing it up, and so we had to
leave it, which was very sad. However, we
sold what remained for nearly seven thousand
pounds; so we did not do so badly. I don't
mean that I got seven thousand pounds out
of it, because, you see, I insisted upon Every
taking a half share. Poor fellow, he had
earned it, if ever a man did. He set up a
store in the old colony on the proceeds, and
did uncommonly well."

"And what did you do with the lion trap?" asked Sir Henry.

"Oh, I brought that away with me also, and when I got to Durban I put it in my house. But really I could not bear to sit opposite to it at nights as I smoked. Visions of that poor woman and the hand of her dead child would rise up in my mind, and also of all the other horrors of which it had been the instrument. I began to dream at last that it had me by the leg. This was too much for my nerves, so I just packed it up and shipped it to its maker in Sheffield, whose name was stamped upon the steel, sending him a letter at the same time to tell him to what purpose the infernal machine had been put. I believe that he gave it to some museum or other."

"And what became of the tusks of the three bulls which you shot? You must have left them at Nala's kraal, I suppose."

The old gentleman's face fell at this question.

"Ah," he said, "that is a very sad story. Nala promised to send them with my goods to my agent at Delagoa, and so he did. But the men who brought them were unarmed, and, as it happened, they fell in with a slave caravan under the command of a half-breed

Portuguee, who seized the tusks, and, what is worse, swore that he had shot them. I paid him out afterwards, however," he added, with a smile of satisfaction; " but it did not give me back my tusks, which no doubt have long ago been turned into hair-brushes!" And he sighed.

"Well," said Good, "that is a capital yarn of yours, Quatermain; but—"

"But what?" he asked, sharply, foreseeing a draw.

"But I don't think that it was so good as mine about the ibex—it hasn't the same *finish*."

Mr. Quatermain made no reply. Good was beneath it.

"Do you know, gentlemen," he said, "it is half-past two in the morning, and if we are going to shoot the big wood to-morrow, we ought to leave here at nine-thirty sharp?"

"Oh, if you shoot for a hundred years, you will never beat the record of those three wood-cock," I said.

"Or of those three elephants," added Sir Henry.

And then we all went to bed, and I dreamed that I had married Maiwa, and was much afraid of that determined lady.

THE END.